HOW TO

Litigate

The Crash Course for Trial Counsel

HOW TO

Litigate

The Crash Course for Trial Counsel

MARTIN L. GRAYSON

DecisionBooks
SEATTLE, WASHINGTON

DecisionBooks is the imprint of LawyerAvenue Press,
a division of Avenue Productions, Inc.

Cover concept by Sandra Imre
Cover and interior design by Rose Michelle Taverniti
Portions of this book were previously published in *The View from the First Chair* (2009)

Volume discounts from LawyerAvenue Press. Email to Books@LawyerAvenue.com, or write to Avenue Productions Inc., 4701 SW Admiral Way #278, Seattle WA 98116.

Library of Congress Cataloging-in-Publication Data

Grayson, Martin L., 1944-
How to litigate : the crash course for trial counsel / by Martin L. Grayson.
pages cm
ISBN 978-0-940675-72-8 (alk. paper)
1. Trial practice--United States. I. Title.
KF8915.G73 2013
347.73'75--dc23

2013000595

For my father

Contents

INTRODUCTION

Who Will Train Tomorrow's Litigators?

In today's world, the need for law firms to generate income to pay for the huge and growing costs of running a legal enterprise creates continuing pressure to bill hours, settle cases, do deals, or otherwise turn time into money.

This reality is magnified by the often large expenditures required for recruiting associates, wining and dining clients, and attending professional conclaves (not to mention the usual costs of running any business). No wonder the idea of training attorneys has faded in importance, weakened by the need to create revenue. As a result, mentoring as a formal exercise is becoming extinct as cases and law firms get larger, and the legal process becomes more specialized and complex. In fact, we have come to a stage where—aside from trial advocacy clinics at some law schools—*there is really no hands-on opportunity for students or young associates to walk into a courtroom other than for the most perfunctory appearances.*

What's more, there are very few, if any, small civil cases on which new attorneys can get trial experience or even full file-handling responsibility.

In most civil cases, the stakes are simply too high for either side to permit a relatively inexperienced attorney to take the case to trial. That is, a substantial case cannot be left in the hands of an associate, no matter how skilled (unless the partner is willing to explain why a case in which the client was assured the damages were no more than $200,000 turned into an adverse judgment for $1.5 million). At the same time, a case with limited damages is often not worth taking to suit, much less trial, so only potentially large cases go to trial, and only partners or very senior associates are permitted to try those cases.

Of course, many attorneys simply learn by doing.

They open a practice straight out of law school or work in a small firm, ostensibly with a "senior" guiding their development. In fact, even in successful firms, the new associate is often just thrown into the water without any instruction to see if he or she has instincts for swimming. Even in large, well-organized firms these days there often is no formal training protocol in how to practice law, and how to prepare and try a case before a jury. One is expected to learn by watching.

Then, if an associate has the desire and ability, and the firm has the need and the inclination, the associate might begin as Second Chair in trial, working with experienced trial counsel.

The job of the Second Chair is to carry the briefcase, i.e., support lead trial counsel, including researching, drafting, filing briefs and Motions (after First Chair has approved); marshaling witnesses; preparing exhibits and having them available in the order required at trial; getting document boxes to the Courtroom; scheduling and sometimes preparing witnesses (most often, secondary witnesses); overseeing the booking and allocation of hotel rooms for staff and witnesses; foraging for food to support the troops; making sure pens and legal pads are at hand; knowing the case inside out and being ready to discuss any issue; proposing arguments and strategies, and making recommendations when asked.

A really good Second Chair is also allowed to examine a witness or two, and a *talented* Second Chair may even get to cross-examine some opposing witnesses.

At some point, the day arrives when the First Chair—the associate's flight instructor—says, "*The aircraft is yours.*" And with that, Second Chair becomes First Chair—lead trial counsel—the lawyer who is instrumental in creating and, solely accountable for, the trial result.

As Second Chair myself back in the 1980s, I tried my first case just 10 months after I was admitted to practice, and two years later, I was First Chair on a number of trials. Now, nearly 30 years after opening my trial practice, I hope that this book (and my *How to Litigate* video series on YouTube) not only offers fresh insight into the litigation process, but also offers some guidance to those of us who venture into the halls of justice to represent our client's causes. Contained in these pages you will find some very practical guidelines for thinking your way effectively and successfully through a lawsuit and, it is my hope, some original instruction in mastering the art.

—*Martin L. Grayson,* Esq., January, 2013

CHAPTER 1

Trial, Day One

You arrive at the Federal Courthouse just after 8:00 a.m.

You have already met with your clients for a working breakfast at their hotel, but you leave after 30 minutes to allow some time and space to yourself. If you are representing plaintiffs, you will have also met with your first witness before 7 a.m., to run through the questioning, but mainly to confirm to the witness that she is ready and in great form.

Your small, wheeled cart hauls two storage boxes and your briefcase. The other items you require, including 16 boxes of exhibits, pleadings, documents, and correspondence, were moved into the courtroom the previous Friday afternoon. For your weekend work (almost 40 hours of it), you needed only copies of the most important exhibits, five deposition transcripts, some verified responses to discovery pleadings and your expert's reports. Your computer, backed up with disks and flash drives, holds all the file documents, including your opening statement, an outline of your probable closing argument (always subject to revision, depending on the testimony and other evidence introduced during the trial), direct and cross examination protocols, and contact numbers for the courtroom and all of your witnesses, including their cell phones and the phone numbers of the hotels where they're staying.

After a small coffee in the cafeteria—during which you glance over documents and quickly review your opening—you note the time: it's now 8:25.

You head for the elevator and ride to the sixth floor, where your clients and first witness are waiting.

Five minutes later, the bailiff opens the door to the courtroom and attorneys file in, lining up to hand the judge's clerk their business cards marked to show the number of their case on the judge's Hearing Docket, and the party represented by the owner of the card. The Clerk advises there are two Motions to be heard before your case will be called. Thirty-five minutes later, the time the judge required to take the bench and dispose of the two Motions, the judge calls your case.

You enter the Well, leaving your cart and storage boxes outside the bar. If you represent plaintiff, you walk to a chair at the counsel table, the one nearest the jury box; if you represent a defendant, you walk to the table furthest from the jury box. You remain standing. The judge calls for appearances, and after plaintiff's counsel states her name and the party she represents, defense counsel does the same. The judge then asks counsel if they are ready to proceed.

To a large extent, the verdict will be based on you.

Your breath catches for a moment, your jaw tenses. You nod confidently and answer clearly: "*The defense is ready, Your Honor.*"

For the next three weeks, the previous 18 months of your life will be on trial.

Of course, you are representing a client, and depending on that client's status and the facts of the case, the key question at trial may be whether or not your client was negligent, whether or not your client breached a contract, whether or not your client committed a criminal act, or whether or not your client suffered a personal injury and, if so, whether or not the negligent or intentional acts of the defendants were the cause of that injury.

But in a very real sense, the jury (or judge if the trial is to the bench), will be deciding how you have done your job.

While deciding the case, the trier of fact will also determine, indirectly, if you have analyzed your case properly and reported it to your client accurately; if you have effectively prepared your witnesses, your exhibits, your opening statement, and closing arguments; if your evidentiary Motions were drafted with care and accuracy based on firm legal tenets; and if you have communicated those elements clearly and logically. The trier of fact will decide if you have organized the facts and evidence of your case into an irrefutable narrative that leads to one conclusion only...in favor of your client.

The members of the jury will rule on the factual issues before them, the judge will rule on legal issues raised during the contest and, at the trial's conclusion, a verdict or Judgment will be rendered.

That verdict, or that Judgment, will tell not only who "won" or " lost" the case (more on that in Chapter 20), it is also a ruling and a judgment on how you have presented your evidence and arguments and conducted yourself as counsel. That ruling will be based not just on one or two witnesses, a few sentences of testimony, or a key piece of evidence; it will be based on your case evaluation, your research of the law, your analysis of the case, and the manner in which you conducted trial. The verdict or judgment will be the result of and, in large part, due to your techniques in deposition, your ability to read and deal with opposing counsel, and the skills you employed in settlement negotiations or plea bargaining. It will reflect your success in thinking through and organizing the myriad facts, numerous legal issues, and many organizational details which comprise a lawsuit and the trial with which that lawsuit, if not settled, must end.

You are trial counsel. To a large extent, the verdict will be based on you.

CHAPTER 2

Depositions

Prior to trial, the most important event in any litigation will occur at deposition; in particular the first deposition you take.

Your preparation, your demeanor, your handling of the facts, legal theories, evidence, and exhibits; the testimony you adduce, the way you handle the witness herself (as well as the way you handle opposing counsel), will all help define your competence, readiness, wit, and confidence in an adversarial setting.

Needless to say, opposing counsel will be an interested observer.

The more competent the opposing counsel, the more closely he or she will be observing you at work and making judgments, perhaps subconsciously, about their chances of out-dueling you in trial. That is not to say your brilliant and careful questioning will outweigh all the facts and all the evidence in a losing cause, and panic the opposing party into withdrawing their lawsuit (if plaintiff) or offering billions in settlement (if defendant). But it will give the opposition pause. Especially if the deponent is a principal in the case, you will be giving his counsel leverage with which to move that party closer to the result you seek. So, given the facts and evidence at hand, you can go a long way toward forcing opposing counsel—and his client—to re-evaluate their chances for success if your performance at deposition is sufficient to raise their respect level for your case and your ability.

The opposite is also true.

Even though a deposition is a formal exercise, an unprepared, uninspired, by-the-book examination tells the witness and opposing counsel you are not to be taken very seriously, much less feared as an adversary.

I have defended depositions in which it was apparent that opposing counsel was intelligent, experienced—perhaps even talented—but unprepared. An attorney willing to take a chance on his ability and talent, without doing his homework, is less to be feared than one who takes the time and makes the effort to fully control his examination. And, by your occasional objection or offhand comment, you will be able to point this out. Interestingly, the more competent the attorney in this situation the more he or she will be aware that you know they are not ready. There are total lunatics in the business who see nothing beyond their own point of view and hear only themselves, but they are still the exception. Most attorneys can gauge the experience and ability of other attorneys rather quickly, and you want them to take you seriously.

How you handle witnesses and opposing counsel defines your competence in an adversarial setting.

For that reason I always wear a suit and tie to deposition. I believe in being friendly, courteous to all, positively jovial when I am defending a deposition, and want everyone as relaxed as possible. But I take the deposition seriously. It's my job, and I take my job seriously. And when I'm on the job, I wear a uniform; a suit and tie, not slacks and a sport shirt.

As for the examination itself, there are dozens of manuals and periodicals, and hundreds, perhaps thousands, of articles and chapters and guides to taking a deposition. In addition to providing general instructions as to form and content, how to advise the deponent of the procedure, giving cautions about perjury (all things you probably already know), there are even form books which tell you exactly what questions to ask of a toxicologist, for example, or an orthopedic surgeon, or an architect, or an economist. For the time being, let's set those aside.

All these guides, like too many attorneys, have a vested interest in appearing to be thorough and in control if not omnipotent, knowledgeable if not omniscient, and beyond surprise if not downright bored with the proceedings. I think most deposition guides, while quite helpful, all overlook one important quality that every truly competent deposition examiner will bring to each deposition.

That quality is...curiosity.

Remember that 1950's sci-fi film, "The Day The Earth Stood Still"? An alien on a special mission arrives on Earth and meets a fearless American scientist. "*You have faith, Dr. Barnhardt,*" says the alien. To which

Dr. Barnhardt replies, "*It is not faith that makes good scientists. It is curiosity.*" And there it is: a line of vintage movie dialogue that goes to the heart of what you need to take a good deposition: curiosity.

In the courtroom, you must be fully prepared for every response a witness might offer, preferably with answers already on the record in the witness' deposition transcript.

But a deposition is a form of pre-trial "discovery," and it is so named for two reasons. All the guides, fact books, and canned deposition treatises are directed to helping you "discover" what the witness is going to say at trial. And that's good. That's why new associates and experienced attorneys alike go into depositions armed with a list of "vital" questions they must not forget to ask. The guides are informative and valuable, and sometimes can point you toward issues you might otherwise overlook. Using the guides will help you discover and record the answer the witness is now bound to give at trial to questions of significance to the issues being adjudicated. The witness either gives the same answer at trial that he gave in deposition or there's lots of explaining to do, none of which is calculated to make the witness look good.

Competent deposition examiners bring curiosity to each deposition.

But while a treatise can explain what witnesses may say—and, in the case of expert witnesses, what the basis of their opinions might be—prepared questions cannot help you discover "why" the witness is going to give those answers. And the "why" is often as important as the "what." And the only way to discover the "why" is with curiosity. "Why" is also the question that most accurately probes witness motive and, thus, helps you interpret all else that is discovered.

Not only does simple curiosity make you a better human being, it makes you more a knowledgeable trial lawyer.

For example, if—as once happened to me—you take the deposition of a railroad bridge watchman, consider it an opportunity to learn things about railroads and bridges, and railroad security and watchmen in general. Not only is it fun, but you might get some very helpful answers for your case, specifically because the witness perceives, perhaps subconsciously, that you are truly interested in what he does and how he does it. As a result, his natural defenses will be lowered.

You can also use genuine curiosity to reduce suspicion and reticence. All witnesses—always, in every case, and without exception—are somewhat defensive and nervous, if not overtly hostile. Defensiveness, along with anxiety, is part of being a witness, often reinforced by the attorney representing him who has probably referred to you, the attorney taking the deposition, if not the process itself, as an instrument of the devil. Every witness is warned, subtly if not blatantly—and believes—he is about to be tortured. Therefore, anything you can do to reduce that tension, that defensive attitude, will stand you and your client in good stead. At the same time, you can not only nail a winning point, but often learn some neat stuff.

All witnesses are defensive and nervous. Reducing that tension helps you and your client.

Even expert witnesses—who are professional testifying machines, supposedly independent, and usually experienced in dealing with the legal process and skilled attorneys—often exhibit the tension and defensiveness that arises when one is "on the spot." Being guarded is a natural posture for any deposition witness: After all, a person is placed under oath, warned about perjury, given admonitions as to how to behave and how to respond, and then treated like a wind-up answering machine.

On the other hand, opening a dialogue in a way that demonstrates the questioner has a genuine interest in learning what the witness has to say and what the witness wants to teach, puts the witness at ease and often elicits much more detailed responses than the simple "yes" or "no" witnesses are instructed to provide wherever possible. In sum, genuine curiosity, especially in technical matters, tends to put even a well-experienced and properly cautious expert witness fully at ease. It makes her feel more in control. You, the examiner, are now on the expert's turf, sitting at the knee of the learned master, begging to absorb his or her wisdom. Why wouldn't they be relaxed? And a relaxed witness is much more likely than a guarded witness to talk himself right into trouble which, in addition to pure "discovery," is not a bad deposition result in itself.

BACK STORY

I once was involved in the defense of a case involving a deck-hand who was severely injured in an oil rig accident in the Gulf of Mexico.

The plaintiff was injured when a wire line, one of many straining to hold a 700,000-pound drill rig, parted and snapped back during the positioning process, striking the plaintiff with lethal force. Plaintiff suffered brain damage, partial paralysis in one arm, and was blinded in one eye. There was no question a lot of money was going to change hands. The only issue was, how much? And more to the point, to what extent did those injuries destroy this person's life?

Seven attorneys representing the various defendants, along with plaintiff's counsel, traveled to Michigan where plaintiff had been treated for more than a year after the accident, to take the depositions of a series of physicians and hospital personnel including plaintiff's psychiatrist. At the time, I was an associate and the most junior of all attorneys present. Accordingly, all five other defense counsel preceded me in asking questions of the psychiatrist over a period of two days. I listened to the psychiatrist's detailed testimony as to diagnosis, treatment, prognosis, evaluation of the plaintiff, opinions as to plaintiff's anticipated rehabilitation, the problems he would face in life, and the potential for his future employment and social adjustment. As you might expect, the psychiatrist did not predict a very happy or productive future for the injured man.

After your questioning, take a break. Let curiosity suggest a follow-up question or two.

When it was my turn to ask questions, there were only a few follow-up issues I wanted clarified in regard to what plaintiff might have said about my client's participation in the activities that led up to the accident. After asking my three substantive questions, my curiosity got the best of me. I was curious about one aspect of the psychiatrist's gloomy predictions concerning the injured man's future.

I wondered if the psychiatrist thought plaintiff's future, setting aside his physical injuries, would have been much brighter without the accident? The initial answer to this question was a bored statement about the impossibility of predicting the outcome of events that did not occur, especially psychological events.

But by now I was really curious, extremely curious. So I persisted.

"Doctor, did you ever ask yourself why the plaintiff—the heir of a wealthy, educated family; a person born and raised in a luxurious Grand Rapids suburb—ended up earning near-minimum wage as a deck-hand on a push-boat working out of Morgan City, Louisiana?"

One of the other attorneys interjected, "*That is a brilliant question*," as the psychiatrist was answering, "*No, I didn't.*"

Personally, I didn't think the question was so brilliant. I just thought it needed asking because I was truly curious. I thought perhaps this might be someone with problems; maybe mental, maybe social, maybe drug- or alcohol-related. But something in the picture didn't fit, and I was curious why.

Later, back at the hotel, the more experienced attorneys in our group had to explain to me just how important that question was to the defense on several different levels. They pointed out that the question cast into doubt that plaintiff's psychological problems were all due exclusively to the accident. But, perhaps more important, they also noted that the psychiatrist's answer suggested she may not have been completely thorough in her appraisal of plaintiff's condition. Moreover, she may have been lazy in obtaining a thorough background, a failure which might even offer grounds to challenge the doctor's competence or, at least, to disparage it in the eyes of the jury.

The lesson I learned that day was that far more experienced and knowledgeable counsel than I had failed to allow simple curiosity to be their friend in the discovery process. All the issues of what, when, and how had been fully explored. But the simple question of "why" plaintiff was the person he seemed to be, was never introduced.

Let's set curiosity aside for now, because in this book good things come in pairs.

As a second deposition "secret," I will reveal one which radio talk-show host Dr. Laura uses with almost every caller to her program: Always stay on point. In the illustration above the psychiatrist had successfully deflected the first question about the deck-hand's probable future. Rather than give up, a second question—this one framed from the perspective of the psychiatrist's procedures—led to the answer we sought.

To stay on point, a good deposition requires energy, endurance, focus, and concentration.

Dr. Laura is a master at staying on point.

A typical on-air exchange might be, "*What can I help you with...*" followed by the caller complaining about all the arguments he is having with his wife, to which Dr. Laura replies, "*But what is the problem you want me to help you with?*" Here the caller complains because he has recommended counseling for his wife, or counseling as a couple, but she refuses. Now, Dr. Laura, starting to lose patience, says, "*If you don't tell me the problem, I can't help and I will hang up.*"

While examiners in deposition don't have the luxury of being curt and dismissive, this technique of ignoring sidetracking comments and staying on the trail of information is one every trial lawyer should take into every deposition. Many interviewers, after hearing the "my-wife-refuses-to-go-to-counseling-with-me" line, would want to know why she refused, whether she had ever been in counseling before, whether the couple had children, how long they had been married, and other information which may or may not be relevant. When the husband finally reveals that his wife has been having an affair with her boss, many other questions become superfluous. So, Dr. Laura is tireless. Dr. Laura does not take, "Okay, but let me tell you something else" for an answer. Dr. Laura is on the case and will not be thrown off the scent.

Neither should you.

Of course, I will also remind you what a number of deposition treatises, and all experienced counsel, will tell you:

Never walk into a deposition without being thoroughly familiar with the law that will control the case and the known facts; at least the facts according to your client. The law is easy to find, in the library or online. For example, a cargo container goes overboard in heavy seas. The "heavy weather" defense is offered. How "heavy" must the weather be to support the defense? The law says the seas must be heavy enough, at the least, to cause some structural damage to the vessel, not just your container. If you walk into the captain's deposition without knowing that precedent, and maybe one or two others about the possibility of course change or anticipated weather and sea conditions given season and location, you may have a pleasant day learning a lot about the horrors of the North Pacific in winter, but you are not going to help your client or your case going forward to trial.

Never walk into a deposition without being familiar with the law that will control the case.

Or, suppose fire destroys $600,000 worth of your client's blue jeans when the factory of the labor contractor where the jeans were being tagged and labeled burns down because of a fire that spread from the auto body shop next door; a fire whose origin was the alley behind the body shop, and probably set by derelicts, according to the Fire Department report and your own expert's analysis. You should, of course, prepare the obvious fact questions about fire prevention and alarm systems in the body shop, and the flammable materials stored there. But you should also know that the law informs us the body shop will not be liable unless there is some independent negligence on its part. Not having a fire alarm system is not, per se, negligence. Storing flammable materials in a workshop is not, per se, negligence.

So what did the body shop do that was negligent? Simply going after the facts may not reveal the answer. But curiosity might.

With a little curiosity about how the fire spread, you might research the law before the deposition, and find that it leads to...weeds. Yes, weeds; uncut dry grass. The fire hazard that the body shop did not abate! In fact, you would even find a section in the Municipal Code, probably unknown to anyone in the employ of the City and never invoked, which allows the City to declare the overgrown storage yard a hazardous condition and public nuisance and, after cutting the weeds, charge the owner/tenant of the property for the work. The County Health & Safety Code, adopted by the city, defines and outlaws weeds and brush as "combustible rubbish" which, in this case, combusted all over your client's blue jeans.

The key to handling delicate testimony... do it last.

So, a curiosity-driven look in the law books before the deposition leads you to ask not only about the non-existent fire alarm (which does not point to negligence), but also to slip in a few questions about how often the body shop owner cuts the grass, and how many lawn mowers he has on the premises. "Oh, none?" you say. "Well, how often does the gardener come around? Oh, you have no gardener?" Well, how about that.

One more point about handling "delicate" testimony: Do it last.

When questioning personal injury plaintiffs, and even experts, you sometimes get responses that bear further inquiry but you know will be uncomfortable for the witness. Two examples:

> One witness, when asked about military service during the early, background-gathering stage of his deposition, stated he had been in the Navy. Asked when he was discharged, and with what sort of discharge, he said, "*General Discharge.*" Because that was not the standard (an Honorable Discharge), it would require further probing. But to do so at that early stage of the deposition would have embarrassed the witness, fueled his resentment and hostility, and increased his defensiveness. I just moved on. Three hours later, looking over my notes before concluding, I returned to the question and asked why he received a General Discharge.
>
> His answer, "*Well, they done an inspection and found heroin in my system.*" Hmmm, heroin. He made it sound like it was a candy bar someone left

in his locker. I had an urge to ask him if he had any idea how it got there, but figured my sarcasm wouldn't play well to that audience.

What is interesting about such testimony is that it achieves a purpose even if the material you find is not admissible at trial, such as felony convictions that do not have to do with credibility. Embezzlement, fraud, or theft might be admissible to show the witness' propensity to lie. An armed robbery conviction would likely not be admissible in a personal injury case to show that the defendant (an armed robber) was negligent. Even though it may not be admissible at trial, the witness knows the behavior was bad and now the witness knows you know; but the witness doesn't know how or when you will use that information. Thus, he might be more inclined to settle reasonably, and less inclined to go to trial and run the risk of a jury finding out someone left heroin in his system, even with his attorney telling him that testimony cannot be used.

A second example:

> Some experts are vulnerable to careful probing of their credentials, an attack which, as noted above, should be reserved for late in the deposition process. Other experts, such as professors at leading universities who are renowned in their fields and whose resumes consist of a 20-page listing of their honors and publications, cannot be challenged in this area. But your local all-purpose "civil engineer" who tailors his resume to make himself look like an expert in building construction defect or products liability can often be made to admit that the resume entry for "Stanford University graduate work" actually consisted of a half-day seminar, and the "professorship" at El Rancho Engineering College is actually a diploma mill he runs out of his garage although accreditation is certain to be obtained in the very near future. As always, simple curiosity is the key that will unlock these doors to the witness' secrets: "*What exactly is El Rancho Engineering College? What is the address? Hmmm, isn't that same address as your house? What courses do you teach? How many students are currently enrolled? How many other 'professors' do you have on the 'faculty.' How much do you charge for an 'engineering' degree?*"

Note-taking during depositions is a personal thing. Some attorneys write down every word uttered by the witness. I do not. We pay the court reporter for that service. But, during the deposition, I will have put an asterisk in the margin of my legal pad next to any point I wish to revisit or, as the witness is speaking, specific answers or questions I may want to pursue later. I do this because I don't want to interrupt the flow of the testimony being developed or to interrupt the current answer. Some points, especially the ones I know will be embarrassing and spark resentment and defensiveness, I leave to pursue late in the deposition at the least delicate moment. That's when you ask, "*Why were you dishonorably discharged from the Navy?*" Not the first thing in the morning.

Simply going after facts may not reveal useful answer... curiosity might.

When you believe you have concluded your questioning, take a break. I will advise the deponent and counsel that I think I am finished but wish to take a moment to look over my notes. While others go out of the conference room to make phone calls, refill their coffee cups, or just take a stretch, take the time to look over your notes to look for asterisks or other symbols you use to signal yourself that there is an area that needs follow-up. And, as important, just think about the areas covered and the case in general. Allow your curiosity to suggest a follow-up question or two. Maybe head to the kitchen for a sip of water just to relax a bit, without particular focus, to see what pops into your mind. Taking a good deposition requires energy, endurance, focus, and concentration. Before closing the proceedings, release that energy and see if a slightly different, internal perspective leads to new thoughts.

A final practice tip

Always get a business card from the court reporter, even your own reporter, at each deposition you attend. I mark mine with the file number and name of the deponent, and then date it and staple it inside the deposition file folder with my notes and exhibits from the day's work. It is rare, but occasionally you will want to contact the reporter to fax over a copy of an exhibit you need to get into the hands of your expert, or perhaps just inquire about when the transcript will be available, or ask why it is delayed. It is very convenient not to have to call opposing counsel for contact information, assuming it was their court reporter. And, even if it is your own reporter, a call to your service will often elicit the query, "Who was your reporter that day?" Unless you know the reporter personally, it is very helpful to have the card handy. It almost always saves time.

CHAPTER 3

Witness Motive

In trial work and in life, one of the most important analyses you can ever make is related to motive.

In order to begin to understand another person, you must first consider what is important to them and what motivates them. Only then can you begin to relate to them realistically in terms of their personality, the behavior they will exhibit, your chances of persuading them to support your goals (personal or professional), and whether you want them as a friend, partner...or your witness at trial.

In the world of the police detective, motive is an overriding theme. For that reason, random crimes, and especially random murders without witnesses, are difficult to solve. Although there are more than five billion people in the world, police investigators start looking for suspects and usually find the perpetrator among the four or five people most closely related to the victim personally or professionally. Occasionally the net must be widened to the neighborhood, or an opposing gang, but in every case the search for a motive will drive the investigation toward a successful conclusion. Find the motive, find the killer. No motive, no killer.

One of the most important steps you can take is to determine witness motive.

Some motives are transparent.

The plaintiff in a personal injury case is motivated to get the highest possible award. The president of a defendant company in a breach of contract action is motivated to avoid all responsibility or liability of any kind for himself and his organization. And, even if it is not expressed openly, it is assumed as a basic tenet of human nature that these individuals, if called as witnesses or in deposition, will give testimony slanted toward achieving their goals even if they would never, ever tell a lie. That is, we expect their motives to be reflected in their testimony.

A skillful trial lawyer will also expect a person's motives to be reflected in and, at the same time, be influenced by their view of reality, their memory, their observations of the world, and the conclusions they draw from the information they perceive and gather. This subconscious molding of reality by internal motive is not only very subtle, it is, by definition, done without conscious decision by the actor. That is, while some witnesses simply lie and know they are lying in their attempt to perpetrate a fraud and escape detection or punishment, others may simply have allowed their wishes, needs, fears, and doubts to so color their view of reality, they are unaware they have done so. A robber knows he committed a crime but tells the jury he did not. We assume such a person, unless he is a complete sociopath, would have trouble passing a polygraph test of his truthfulness about his involvement in the crime.

Some witnesses let their wishes, needs, fears, and doubts color their view of reality.

But what about the worker, a personal injury plaintiff injured as a result of his own negligence? He forgot to check a gas bleed valve on the oil well drill rig before he began his welding work. That oversight, coupled with a welding spark and the failure of the valve to function as designed because it was not completely closed, resulted in an explosion that injured several workers and caused extensive property damage. Now, our plaintiff has been on the job for 20 years, he's checked hundreds perhaps thousands of bleed valves in his day. He swears under penalty of perjury he checked the valve although, in fact, he cannot actually recall doing so. We know for certain he did not check it (or, if he did, he failed to notice the valve was partially open). But is he lying? I suggest that this witness might well pass a polygraph test, unlike the thief claiming innocence in our example above. The reason is, he is not telling a lie that contradicts truth in his own mind.

He is simply allowing his motive for testifying to shape his reality.

For the same reason, it is not uncommon for multiple witnesses to the same casualty to have varying recollections of the event. Sometimes witness statements and recollections are widely variant and wholly contradictory. Are all these witnesses lying? I think not. I believe there are several variables accounting for such differences. Those variables range from simple misunderstanding of events arising, perhaps, from faulty observation or inattention to the most important of all—*witness motive.*

BACK STORY

Years after I began the practice of law at a mid-sized firm specializing in maritime and oil and gas litigation, I tried cases, deposed witnesses, evaluated witness testimony, and reported my analyses to senior partners and clients without ever considering *witness motive* other than the obvious—plaintiffs always want to get as much money as possible, and defendants want to avoid paying any money at all.

Then I met someone I'll call "Canoe Ranger."

Now, this story is a bit detailed, but it will tell you something important about witness motive.

The case involved a woman who worked as an offshore gauger/switcher for an oil field contractor. Her job was to go from one production platform to another in the Gulf of Mexico, measuring hydrocarbon production, switching valves, recording product levels, and inspecting various pieces of equipment. She traveled from rig to rig on small crew boats, usually manned by a skipper and a deck-hand. She claimed to have fallen on such a vessel, severely injuring her back, spending most days in a wheelchair, and was able to walk only short distances with the aid of crutches. When, in deposition, I asked her what she was doing with her time since her injury, she said she was taking courses at a junior college, hoping a better education would allow her return to the job market in an office environment because she did not think she could ever work offshore again. Gutsy, smart, admirable. A jury was going to love her, and probably award her enough money so she wouldn't ever have to work again anywhere.

Everyone has motive for their actions no matter how subtle or unrecognized.

Because I was curious, though, I learned the name of the junior college she attended in Texas, and subpoenaed her transcript. In reviewing it, I noticed a canoeing course plaintiff had taken to satisfy a physical education requirement.

When I phoned her instructor, he turned out to be a pleasant, well-spoken state park ranger who taught the course as an adjunct. My "Canoe Ranger" said he only vaguely recalled plaintiff and her canoeing class, and he said he didn't believe he could be much help. Indeed, the information he provided was imprecise and fairly insignificant. It seems that most of the instruction was held in a classroom, and he could not recall whether plaintiff got around in a wheelchair or on crutches.

He did remember, however, that one session was held at the campus swimming pool so that the class could demonstrate what they had learned in real canoes.

Canoe Ranger said he believed plaintiff participated in that class as it was a course requirement, but that he could not actually swear she did as he had no independent recollection. Even if she had been in the pool, however, plaintiff had already testified she had friends help her get around when necessary, so I anticipated she could explain away what I had first hoped was a chance to show she was not as incapacitated as she claimed.

We listed Canoe Ranger as a trial witness, explaining that I might call him at trial and would put him under subpoena to make it easier for him to get time off and his expenses reimbursed. When opposing counsel inquired about the unrecognized name listed as a witness, I explained, as an attorney is obligated to do. A few days later, opposing counsel called to say he had spoken to his client and thought Canoe Ranger would be a waste of time. He told me what I already knew, that the course consisted mainly of classroom work, and what I suspected, that for the one pool session, plaintiff was assisted by friends.

Still, we called Canoe Ranger as a trial witness if only to demonstrate to the jury that plaintiff was far from helpless, and was not doomed to a life of pain and immobility even though I assumed she would testify that she was able to complete the pool exercise only on her very best and most active day, after having taken loads of pain killers in advance, but that she suffered for weeks afterward with no one around to witness her agony.

As it turned out, Canoe Ranger was the all-time heavyweight champion of witnesses. He was a third-party with absolutely no personal or professional involvement in the lawsuit. From the jury's point of view, he was a man to be believed; a likeable young park ranger with nothing personal at stake. He also happened to be the best witness I ever had, expert or percipient. He was the Mr. Universe of witnesses.

Apparently, after I first contacted him, Canoe Ranger went back through his class notes and records that included enrollment forms provided by the college. There in his file, he noticed copies of waiver forms from a class field trip, a rare event he held for this particular canoeing class because it was such an agreeable group, because it was the right time of year, and because he had recently broken up with his fiancée and had plenty of free time.

Canoe Ranger was then able to recall that plaintiff participated fully; that is, she portaged (carried) her canoe like everyone else, slept on the ground in a tent, paddled and walked and gathered fire wood, prepared food and sang around the campfire, just like all the other students. And then right in the middle of his testimony, he held up to the jury a group photo (*"That's her in the red baseball cap"*). Of course, the photo was immediately excluded, correctly, as objectionable because I had not known the picture existed and did not have it on the exhibit list. The jury, of course, was told by the judge to ignore the photo as if it never existed. Right. But the jury heard plenty about that picture, because even though we were not allowed to show it to them, it is within the rules to have the witness describe the picture and the field trip, and that I had him do at length. I asked so many questions about that field trip and that photograph, the jury must have dreamed about it for years afterward. And the best part was, Canoe Ranger, as a third party, had no apparent interest in the lawsuit. Neither he nor his college was even mentioned as possible defendants for they had nothing whatsoever to do with plaintiff's alleged injury. So the jury, and I, believed every word he said and the impression he gave without question.

He was unimpeachable.

But when something is too good to be true, it usually isn't.

I began to wonder why Canoe Ranger did all that homework before coming into Court. Why, after sounding so neutral when I first interviewed him, did he conduct such an ardent search for the truth? That's when I realized he had…a motive. It's also when I understood that *everyone* has a motive for their actions, no matter how subtle or unrecognized.

Canoe Ranger's motive was actually quite simple.

My phone call, which gave him only minimal facts about the case and plaintiff's claims, started him thinking that he, and maybe the college, too, had permitted an unfit student to participate in an activity that might have been too strenuous. And while he doubted the activity would cause injury, it might well have exacerbated her pre-existing injuries. Though I never asked him about it, I imagined that, perhaps, in the dark of night after our first conversation, Canoe Ranger worried that, even though a proper waiver form had been signed, just maybe, he and the college had not been diligent in confirming all students were physically able to participate in the course.

When you ignore witness motive, you may be in for an unpleasant surprise.

Canoe Ranger's motive was to protect himself and the college from any inference that they were not being fully responsible.

Even though there was no such claim, and even though I believe he was probably not aware of his own motive, I am convinced it guided his actions and his testimony. In fact, if I had thought of it earlier, my preparation of this witness would have touched on how students are screened to make sure they are physically capable of completing the course, that the college is always concerned about student well-being and would never allow a person who might be at risk for injury to engage in a strenuous physical activity, and that the waiver form is taken very seriously and explained to each student along with a description of trip activities and requirements. Instead, I must confess, this line of questioning never occurred to me. If it had, I could have confirmed the procedures taken by Canoe Ranger and the school, and reinforced the testimony he would give even though it turned out to be unnecessary.

Now, of course, such preparation always occurs to me, because I learned the lesson of the Canoe Ranger and I fully believe, as noted above, that *everyone has a motive for their testimony as well as for their actions, or failure to act* (even laziness, like other personality traits, can impact motive).

A skilled attorney will want to determine those motives in order to understand the witness and control the presentation. When you ignore *witness motive,* you may be in for an unpleasant surprise, as was plaintiff's counsel in the case of the Canoe Ranger.

CHAPTER 4

Preparing Your Witness

When it comes to preparing witnesses for deposition, you have several goals.

First and foremost, and even before you explain what a deposition is and why theirs is being taken, you must instruct every witness to tell the truth. You want that embedded in your witness's memory bank. It is the perfect answer to the many snide, usually objectionable, questions that are the last resort of an examiner who is being buried by a well-prepared witness.

"*Just what did you think your job was here today?*" is best answered by the witness saying, "*I thought I was supposed to tell the truth,*" as opposed to your jumping in with, "*Objection, argumentative, bad manners, impolite.*"

Remember, too, for witnesses you may be preparing who are NOT your client, or not your client's employees or agents, there is no attorney-client privilege for your discussions. And for these occasional witnesses, who can not invoke the attorney-client privilege, I can tell you from personal experience that you will never hear a more satisfying response to the question, "*...And in your meeting with Mr. Grayson earlier today, what did he tell you to say?*" than, "*He told me to tell the truth.*" Smile, smile. No objection.

You want your witnesses to tell the truth as quickly as possible in the shortest possible form

In fact, truth is good and you ought to advise all witnesses to tell the truth. At the same time, there are ways of *revealing* the truth that may be more or less helpful to your cause, and that is why you are preparing the witness in the first place.

For one thing, you want your witnesses to tell the truth as quickly as possible, in the shortest possible form.

I warn witnesses that if they give an attorney a one-minute answer, they'll get 10 minutes of follow-up questions. So, if they give an attorney a one-second answer, they may have 10 seconds of follow-up. I explain to witnesses that, due to this reality, they really are in control of the proceedings, and it is up to them to decide which situation they would rather face. The witness always gets the message. Most witnesses even quickly volunteer the conclusion I want them to reach.

"*So, I should answer yes or no?*" There you go, yes or no…whenever you can.

Which raises another important point: You want the witness to discover for himself what you are trying to explain. Remember, you are not telling the witness what to say. In the process of asking the witness to clarify your understanding, to explain certain details, to recall certain circumstances, however, you can massage a memory. If you ask a witness directly, "*Where were you looking at the time of the explosion,*" the answer will probably be, "*I don't recall.*" It is much more effective to ask, "*So, based on what you have said you were preparing to do, it is likely you were looking in the direction of the fuel tank when you heard the boom,*" or, "*Is it possible you were looking at the generator when you heard the sound? You do recall seeing the generator around the time of the explosion?*"

It may be important to your case to have some evidence that the generator was not the point of origin of the explosion. So, if your witness can reveal any information that it was intact at the time she heard the boom, you want to test that premise thoroughly and before the witness has committed to saying he doesn't recall.

Truth is good, but there are ways of revealing it that may be more or less helpful to your cause

Then, later, after the witness has clarified where he was looking, you can come back and reinforce the message. "*Earlier you said you were likely looking in the direction of the fuel tank, correct? And, if I recall the scene, that would have been right out in front of the production platform where you were standing?*"

The reason it's important to reinforce the memory is because it might otherwise appear to be weak, perhaps even directed testimony. Such testimony never stands up under good cross-examination because it is based on little more than the witness's instinct to please his employer or counsel. Such poorly prepared witnesses can always be led into contradicting their earlier statements because they themselves are not ready to defend grounds that others have provided. The vital part of witness preparation is having the witness adopt your client's view as his own, assuming always he can do so honestly. A simple instruction to do so is not only unethical, it is never effective.

Introducing the Lifeline

The single most important aspect of witness preparation is to provide the deponent with what I call the Lifeline.

Lifelines are an established radio talk-show technique that employs a memorized, all-purpose phrase to get you through a tough situation. Talk show host Dr. Laura makes good use of the Lifeline technique. Whenever one of her callers gets out of hand, she reaches for her own "lifeline". It's usually something like, "... *Don't have babies.*" For your witness, of course, the Lifeline is not the opportunity for a glib put-down but rather the one point you want your witness to drive home to help your case. And it should be used in response to any question that makes the witness feel trapped, uncomfortable, or unwilling to give a direct response. In short, the Lifeline is the answer that moves the discussion back to where the witness has the advantage.

Poorly prepared witnesses can always be led into contradicting their earlier statements.

Expert witnesses make especially good use of Lifelines. The one bullet that all skilled expert witnesses have locked-and-loaded is the ability to deflect a question that puts them on the defensive. They do this by using their own Lifeline to go on the offensive.

For example, consider an expert economist who has not been able to analyze all relevant records in a case: In response to the obvious question, "*You have not analyzed all of ABC Company's financial reports, have you Dr. Smoothy?*" the Lifeline is, "*Those reports were never made available.*"

Now, a focused examiner would stay on point and ask, "*Regardless of the reason, it is true you have not analyzed the financial reports, correct?*"

Again, the witness can invoke their Lifeline in another form: "*I would be happy to analyze any records that are provided to me; that's what I do.*"

The witness is still not answering the question while, at the same time, implying the opposition is trying to hide the truth. Eventually, the expert may have to admit, "*Well, as soon as those records become available, I would be happy to analyze them but, no, I haven't been able to analyze them yet.*" By the time the examiner has scored his point, though, it is weakened, deflated and, finally, only delivered when it is all wrapped up in the Lifeline that explains it away.

As I mentioned earlier, the Lifeline is the one message you provide—from the witness's knowledge—that moves the testimony in the direction you want it to go. It's the answer to give when a more direct answer might hurt your case. Every witness, in every case, in every situation, has a position that they wish to state and defend. Once you have determined what the Lifeline is, you must teach your witness how and when to use it. Only then will they be fully prepared for deposition; relaxed, confident, and less afraid of the traps, tricks, and pitfalls that await.

With a Lifeline, a witness will be less afraid of the traps, tricks, and pitfalls that await.

Remember "Canoe Ranger" from the previous chapter?

If he had been asked the one question which might have weakened his compelling testimony, i.e., "*Isn't it true you never asked Plaintiff if she was physically capable of undertaking all the required class activities?*" he has a choice of answers. He can answer, "*Yes, that's true,*" conceding the point and weakening his testimony. Needless to say, that is not the result we wanted.

You want the witness to protect your case and themselves. You want Canoe Ranger to say…

> "*Determining physical ability is really up to the person taking the course. If a participant has physical issues, he should point them out to the instructor or the administration. It is impossible for the school to know each group member's physical fitness or limitation at any given moment. That's why we require the waiver forms. These are adults who know and understand their situation better than I ever could. Obviously, I'm not a doctor. Of course, as soon as we are advised of an issue, we do everything we can to accommodate every class member's needs so it is very important for the participant to give us that information.*"

Now that's a Lifeline a witness can believe in. And a lot better for your case than, "*Gee, I never thought of asking.*"

In the context of preparing the witness, you need only ask, "*Canoe Ranger, would it be possible for you to determine the physical abilities of each class member? Are you qualified to do that? But if a student told you they had a problem, you would do whatever you could to help them out and protect them, right?*"

Witness demeanor is another consideration that must be covered in preparation.

As suggested earlier, you must persuade the witness that they control the deposition. Just as we have discussed being cordial and friendly to all, your witnesses must maintain an open, friendly attitude no matter how stressful or contentious the deposition becomes. I am always pleased when a witness I am deposing becomes testy and argumentative. It means the witness is being pressed and is anxious. It means we are scoring points and, just as important, the witness is losing control of his emotions and is more likely to tell me what I want to hear. Just as the expert who believes you are genuinely interested in his field is more likely to let down his guard and mention some minuses along with the pluses, so, too, is an agitated witness more likely to give testimony damaging to his cause.

Your own witnesses, on the other hand, must always remain calm and cordial.

If you see your witness losing patience, take a break during which you should tell them how well they are doing, especially in light of the unfair, lowdown, dirty tactics being used by examining counsel. You are proud of them for not falling onto the trap of losing their cool. They should just keep right on being truthful and calm and the other side will learn their lesson and bring matters to a close. Lose your cool and you might be here all day, into the night, and sitting in that same conference room tomorrow. The witness will get the message.

A final word to your witness on filling in blanks: A time-tested interrogation technique makes use of silence. Witnesses often feel a need to fill empty space with sound; their sound, their talk. This is not good. Your witness should be prepared to wait, silently, politely, until the examiner asks a question. There is no need for the deponent to continue talking just because the examiner is trying to think of a follow-up to the last response.

BACK STORY

One of the best questions I believe I ever asked in deposition turned on a single word. The case involved a predawn *allision* (i.e., striking a fixed object) involving a heavily loaded, 395-foot barge and a bridge over Florida's Apalachicola River. The bridge was out in the boondocks, and illuminated only with diesel lanterns. The bridge-keeper, who was supposed to open the swing span whenever he heard a whistle signal from a tug, had a portable generator set up to run a heater and a television for those cold nights when he had nothing to do for hours but sit in front of a picture window looking out at the river, waiting for the one or two tugs that might transit between 11 p.m. and 7 a.m.

Our tug captain testified that he blew the signal but the bridge never opened, although it appeared to be opening as the tug-and-tow slid around a bend to line up on the channel. The tug almost stopped in time but tapped the bridge just hard enough to throw the span and the train tracks four feet east of where they needed to be. It took more than 200 men, six barges, and three weeks to support and lift the bridge and replace it in position.

The railroad suing the tug company I represented claimed that the tug never sounded its whistle and that the tug captain, a new employee traversing that portion of the river for the first time at night, didn't realize until too late that the bridge was ahead. Indeed, the bridge tender claimed, quite early in his testimony, he never heard a whistle.

Late in the day, when I was almost finished with my examination, I asked the bridge-keeper if it got cold in that little bridge-tender's shack at night in February, and he conceded it did.

I asked if it got lonely out there on the river, middle of the night, nothing on television, sitting in his rocking chair in front the heater. He conceded it did get lonely.

I asked him if he ever fell asleep in that rocking chair and he immediately answered, "*No, I don't.*"

A little worn out from travel, and seven hours of asking questions, probing, and battling, I bowed my head toward the conference table and paused. Unable to think of any piercing challenge to what I sincerely believed was a lie, I tilted up to look up at the witness from table level and shaking my head, whispered, begged, "*Never* (fall asleep)?"

"*Well,*" he said, "*I don't make a habit of it.*"

Oh, big mistake. He had already answered the question, and he should never have tried to answer a second time.

Afterward, the federal judge who heard the case ruled a 60-40 split of liability in a case where only one participant, my client, was moving at the time of the incident.

The lesson: You don't want your witness to fill a silence; you don't want them to volunteer. And you certainly don't want them volunteering to fill in the blanks in testimony that should remain blank.

Question: "*Did you have lunch on September 16, 2011?*"

The correct answer is NOT, "*I'm sure I did*," or "*Probably,*" or—worst of all—"*Yes, because I have lunch every day.*"

The correct answer is, *"I don't recall."*

Your witness needs to understand that he or she cannot speculate.

If they do not have specific recall and memory of an event, they must admit they do not know or do not recall. It can be a terrible setback when a witness's credibility is marred by an innocuous admission made only because the witness was trying to be helpful.

Witnesses often become flustered if they do not have clear answers to questions. They begin to let the suggestions of counsel lead them astray and, what's worse, assume some things happened not because they truly recall them happening, but because those things happen so routinely it is just assumed they happened in the current case. Many witnesses are also embarrassed and quickly tire of repeating, *"I don't recall."* And in response to the question—*"Did you have lunch on September 16, 2011?*—they may also fear looking foolish for not being able to remember such a common event.

In fact, the mundane nature of the event is what makes it difficult to remember. It is only in retrospect—AFTER the explosion—that the time the witness took her lunch break becomes important, perhaps vital to the case. At the time that lunch break was actually occurring, there was no case, there was no explosion; there was just another workday, another lunch, like thousands of others.

Witnesses feel a need to fill a silence with talk. This is not good.

The Lifeline that your witness can use in these circumstances is what we shall call the "just-another-day" Lifeline.

In preparing the witness, you might ask an innocuous question that you expect the witness would not be able to answer. For example, you might ask if, perhaps, they were a little early to work two weeks ago Tuesday or if they were right on time. You might ask the color of the tie they wore that day or what color purse they carried. When they look at you with an odd slant of the head, or tell you there is no way to remember such detail, you agree.

"That's right," you tell them. *"You don't know. And you probably don't recall because it was just another day. Until the explosion, you had no idea you were going to be summoned as a witness two years later, and asked to recall little details of that day. You did not know what was going to take place or perhaps you would have kept notes. But on an ordinary day you don't need notes to remind you where you had lunch, or even if you had lunch at all. And before all this happened it was just an ordinary day."*

Advise the witness that they can point that fact out to counsel, and especially to one who seems to be getting testy because they cannot recall the details she wants them to confirm. I've had witnesses say something along the lines of, "*Heck, if it wasn't for that explosion, I couldn't even have sworn I went to work that day…wouldn't have had a reason to remember.*"

A trial mini-lifeline should be provided to witnesses, especially expert witness, in the form of a subpoena. While everyone knows that expert witnesses are paid to testify and that other witnesses are, at the least, entitled to reimbursement of expenses, many attorneys still attempt to embarrass witnesses with those facts. The mini-lifeline is provided by making certain to subpoena your own witnesses, especially experts. That allows a perfect answer to the sneering, disdainful question of opposing counsel, "*You are getting paid to testify here today, aren't you Dr. Smoothy?*" The answer: "*I am testifying here today because I am under subpoena to testify. But I am honored to appear and tell the truth to the best of my ability.*"

CHAPTER 5

How to Beat a Bully

Practice law long enough (say, more than a month), and you will end up in deposition with one or more loud, obnoxious, rude, rule-trampling, witness-coaching, usually foul-mouthed opposing counsel. This lawyer's idea of defending a deposition—even when the deponent is not his witness—is to object to every question with long and loud complaints and protests, including explanations of what the question should have been, what the answer should be, and why everyone's time is being wasted by your questioning.

I have noticed that, over the years, these characters seem to be diminishing in number. So, perhaps there is a new day dawning in civility and competence. Then again, perhaps not. I am told by younger practitioners that these clowns are still out in force and, if anything, may be growing in number and stridency. Perhaps there is a correlation. Perhaps, like many predators, the bully tends to prey on the weak, which is how he perceives the younger, more courteous, and less experienced attorney.

So, assuming you are, in fact, polite, professional, and a bit new at the game, how do you deal with the gorilla in a tie pretending to be a lawyer?

Be polite when dealing with the gorilla in a tie pretending to be a lawyer.

Above all, be polite.

Do not, under any circumstances stoop to any act or word with less than scrupulous courtesy and dignity, especially so long as you are on the record. You are about to cage and subdue the ape, but you can do so only with the most gentle of techniques. Any act or sign of aggression will not only fuel the fire, it will render you weaponless. For in the battle with the uncouth, you have the high ground and the winning hand only so long as you are untouched by rancor. Not even a mild touch of bemused sarcasm should cross your mind or your lips.

As the drama unfolds, be certain the record, i.e., the deposition transcript, has all your comments to counsel, lauding his efforts to assist his client, apologizing if all your questions are not all perfectly phrased, commenting how nice it is you all are gathered together on that day with the common purpose of seeking the truth. You might request counsel's cooperation in that enterprise, and voice your disapproval of his methods. But do so as gently and courteously as possible. Know also, that being well prepared, staying on point and unflustered, despite counsel's miserable behavior, is the first antidote to such behavior, and often all that is required to return the enterprise to more civil and effective territory.

Experience has taught me that when there is no payoff for the bad behavior, it tends to diminish.

At the same time, do not be dismayed if counsel's outbursts continue, even escalate, as he realizes you will not be sidetracked into arguing over his objections. You are baiting a trap here and may even take the opportunity to help counsel paint himself into a corner. Interrupt a tirade to ask if he is instructing the witness not to answer. If so, and unless the information requested is clearly privileged, counsel will be on shaky ground indeed. Ask the court reporter to mark such instructions separately and clearly for later retrieval and move on. If there is no instruction not to answer, have the court reporter repeat the question. Occasionally, you may wish to rephrase a question for clarity and, in general, you will want your questions to be short, simple, clear, precise, and as short as possible. Did I mention your questions should be short?

If your calm, courteous demeanor doesn't have the desired effect, go to Plan B.

If necessary, ask three short, simple questions instead of the one you might normally ask in a different setting. You are trying to establish a clear record of professional focus and dignity, and you should give the opposition no wiggle room for objections as to the form of the question.

If the deposition proceeds at this level, so be it. It may take longer than it should, but you will get your testimony.

Now, at some point, if your calm, courteous demeanor has not had the desired effect on the rampaging moose, it is time to go off the record.

Ask for a word in private with counsel. Be sure you are well away from the witness and any other counsel or attendees; in other words, not just on the other side of the conference room's glass wall. The old days when you could call the Court and expect to get a judge or a proactive law clerk on the line to set things right are gone, at least in the major metropolitan jurisdictions where most of this nonsense occurs. So, you will have to use Plan B, that you now explain to counsel as follows:

- You are going to continue the deposition, asking questions as carefully as you can.
- If counsel continues his obstructive behavior, you are going to ask him one more time to stop and let the process proceed in good faith.
- If he refuses, you are going to adjourn the deposition, and are going to bring a Motion, based on the record, and ask the judge not only to order an end to his rude, improper, and obstructive behavior, you are going to seek sanctions for the time and effort involved in the Motion as well as making counsel responsible for all costs of the continued deposition, including transcripts.

Explain to counsel you are taking this step only as a last resort. You would like everyone to get along and finish up in good order. And maybe the judge will decide counsel is acting properly and professionally and will frown on your Motion. You are willing to take that chance. But you are not willing to proceed as you have been forced to do for the past hour. Once again, request counsel's cooperation. Ask, can we be friends and get this deposition completed and go home to our families? Smile, nod, firm handshake, pat on the back.

When dealing with the uncouth, you hold the winning hand if you are untouched by rancor

This tactic is 98 percent guaranteed to change the entire tone of the proceedings.

For the two percent of the cases where this does not work, you should ask a few more questions, get counsel's ridiculous objections on the record, and then adjourn the deposition, giving the same recitation on the record that you gave counsel in private, even mentioning that your last, off-the-record, conference advised counsel you would have no choice but to take this step. At this point, it will be opposing counsel calling for an "off-the-record" discussion begging you not to adjourn. This assumes he realizes—as all but the most rabid do—that he has been set up and will not be treated gently by any judge who has to read this record.

It will be your choice whether or not to allow him to persuade you to continue.

You see now why it is so important to be calm, courteous, focused, and professional throughout the ordeal. You may now walk into court with clean hands and pure thoughts, presenting the judge with a clear record, registering your dismay that counsel could not resolve the matter among themselves, but pleading with the Court to let the justice system do its job as intended, which means letting you take the deposition and asking your questions in any manner you choose subject of course, to the Court's later ruling on any legitimate objection.

You will not lose this Motion.

And, in addition to letting opposing counsel know who is in charge, and perhaps even getting some expenses reimbursed for your client, you will have educated the Court as to who is the good guy and who is the bad guy. There are, in fact, very few counsel, no matter how disturbed or incompetent, who are dumb enough to let themselves get ambushed into this position but it does occur. You will probably have carried the day and taken your deposition long before this point. But, as always, when you act with clean hands and pure intention, never hesitate to put your actions before the Court.

Righteousness in the service of the law, and your client—in addition to being its own reward—is often a great deal of fun. It is also a pleasure every once in a while to pick up a stick and smite the wicked. With great courtesy, of course.

CHAPTER 6

Managing Your Case

The brain is a finite reservoir. It switches between thoughts at lightning speed, but can hold only one thought at a time.

Don't believe me? Try this:

> Divide a deck of playing cards into two stacks. Now, count the first stack as rapidly as you can. It should take less than 10 seconds. Now, do the same with the other stack, this time counting spades *at the same time* you're counting cards.

I doubt you can do it accurately or quickly without practice. That's because the brain, as quick as it is, works in linear fashion. It does one thing at a time.

One of the attributes of all good attorneys is the ability to carefully manage the massive amounts of documentary material they must master in any large or complicated case or transaction. Notice, I said *manage.* I didn't say memorize, I didn't say learn, I didn't even say understand. I said *manage.* My point is that, since you can only do one thing—or think one thought—at a time, and since you have massive numbers of thoughts and things to handle including new files, documents, phone messages, court hearings, client conferences, witness prep, lunch, and depositions, you must find a way to manage these things efficiently, and ensure that not even one little item gets overlooked.

Because that one little thing will usually be the one that makes it necessary for you to have malpractice insurance.

A personal example

One of my great victories as a second-year associate concerned document management. And it earned me the undeserved reputation as a document wizard with a photographic memory.

The case involved a $12 million shipment of coffee from Madagascar to the Dutch port of Rotterdam with a stopover in New Orleans. Thousands of bags were delivered in a condition unfit for consumption, and the lawsuit that followed generated an exceptionally large amount of paperwork befitting a shipment on seven different vessels to two different countries.

> **Everyone wanted to know my secret for handling so much paper.**

In addition to all the cargo documents (inquiries, quotations, product specifications, purchase orders, sales receipts, packaging details, bag markings, inspections), and all the vessel documents (bridge logs, hatch receipts, loading particulars, stow plans, manifests, temperature records, engine room logs, inspection reports), there were customs documents, survey reports, freight forwarders' records, all the correspondence among all the parties, not to mention the largest single group of documents, that generated by the claim itself, including notices, reports, demands, damage surveys, and correspondence with copies of notices and transmittals of all the other documents. In sum, more than 7,000 numbered exhibits—consisting of nearly 100,000 pages—were generated by plaintiff and seven defendants, each of whom was represented by a different law firm.

My secret revealed

The defense group was led by a large firm, of whom lead counsel was a senior partner we all called Duke. I was the youngest, newest attorney in my firm (and the most junior in the room). For one of the depositions I was allowed to attend on my own, I remember my boss instructing me to shut up, listen carefully, and to help Duke any way I could. A few hours into the deposition of one of the freight forwarders, Duke referred to a pre-loading inspection report that detailed the condition of the cargo as showing evidence of some wetting, moisture, or condensation. One of the attorneys asked Duke which document he was referring to and, as Duke started sorting through piles of paper, I said quickly, "*Document number 787.*"

Duke looked at me for a moment and nodded.

The deposition continued. Later, Duke made reference to a survey report to which I chimed in correctly, "*Document number 2316.*"

Still later, Duke referred to another document. This time he paused and looked in my direction. Again, I offered the correct exhibit number.

After the deposition, word spread around the firm about my mastery of the avalanche of documents in the *Adriana* case. Everyone wanted to know my "secret" for handling so much paper. Secret? There was no secret. Everybody, Duke included, should have known exactly what I knew: Of the 7,281 exhibits in the file, only 16 of them were really important. My only secret was having extracted those 16, and read or glanced through each of them. If someone had asked me for the *Gorgio II Stow Plan,* I would have been fumbling around just like everyone else. But if they were looking for the *Davis & Gale Survey Report,* it was in Folder #3 right in front of the file!

A system is essential

So, what would you do with that Marine Surveyor's Report analyzing the damage sustained by the contents of a cargo container dropped from a height of four feet onto the bed of a flatbed chassis by a gantry crane at the port? After reading the report, you can throw it on your desk, where it might lay for months (maybe years), and encounter it from time to time, spending less and less time with it as you come to recognize what it is and realize you don't need it...yet. Or, you can drop the Report into a catchall "*Client Documents*" folder in your file along with bills of lading, manifests, invoices, packing lists, delivery receipts, stowage plans, ship logs, weather reports, correspondence, deposition transcripts, claim files, and perhaps several other survey reports.

How many times will you skim past the same document looking for another?

Either way, you are guaranteeing you will get to read that report or, at the very least, scan the cover page, several dozen times over the next year while looking for other things. What's more, you will have to rummage through each pile of documents every time you want to find the Surveyor's Report; whether to check a certain fact for a deposition, report a detail to the client, view a photograph it contains, review it prior to adding it to your trial exhibit list and, later, review it in depth prior to witness preparation and trial. This situation isn't unique.

In any commercial case with large value, the number of documents may well be in the thousands, and the number of pages in the tens or even *hundreds* of thousands. So, for every day you don't have a system to manage your documents, how many times will you skim past one document looking for another? How many minutes—hours—will you waste trying to find a document you had in your hand just three days earlier?

What to do? Have a system, and manage your life.

My own system is quite simple.

After reading the ABC Survey Report, I grab a Manila folder and mark the file number on the tab with a short note describing the contents. I use simple notes that read something like, "*2356 ABC Survey*." Even though the complete file number may be 0267-06-2356, the last four digits in our office are exclusive to one file only. Shorter is better. You're going to read this tab a number of times before the case goes to trial. It's tough on your eyes, and your brain, if, every time you look through the file for a document, you have to decipher that file tab reading "0267-06-2356 ABC Survey Report received on 9/6/05 relating to container damage aboard the M/V WEATHER BIRD in the North Pacific on 3/12/05." Much better to read, "*2365 ABC Survey*."

Our four-digit document code system is also very convenient for billing.

I do like to note the "ABC," however, because the same casualty might later generate an "XYZ Survey" and, in large cases with several parties, there may well be a number of different survey reports, all of which will be read when received, placed in a folder marked with the file number, and placed in the file to remain, forever after, readily available to one and all, at a glance.

Moreover, in our office, while the first six digits of a file number are coded for the client and the year opened, the last four digits are an exclusive identifier used only one time. And so long as we don't start opening more than 9,999 files a decade, we shouldn't have to worry about the confusion of repeating file numbers. Our system, using the exclusive four-digit code, is also very convenient for billing in-house charges like express courier fees and tracking outside services. It also simplifies filing and reduces filing error.

Compare this simple system to the one used in many offices, where the code is based on a "*client number/file number*" description such as 023-01, 023-02, 023-03, etc. As you can imagine, this system quickly becomes a mess when you eventually have a client 032, and their files will be numbered 032-01, 032-02, 032-03. Eventually, you'll have client number 123 with files 123-01, 123-02, and a then a client 231 with 231-01, 231-02, etc. Maybe this won't confuse the attorneys who are hands-on with these files; who know the contents (and probably think of the file by a name such "the WEATHER BIRD file," rather than a number). But it is a disaster for support staff. Thus, it shouldn't be surprising that in some law offices there are almost as many documents misfiled as are filed correctly.

But if you have a good system ...

Once the "*2356 ABC Survey Report,*" is neatly tucked into its Manila folder within the master file, you never have to see it again until you need it to depose the surveyor, review the contents for a report to client, compare it to a new report for consistency, or for any other purpose. In other words, one's limited brain function never has to waste time even glancing at the ABC Survey Report again, unless you specifically want to do so. An added benefit of this system is that I'm not the only one who knows where the report may be buried on my desk. Any colleague, paralegal, or staff member, can go to the file and pull the ABC survey report in a few moments. Later, when this case goes to trial, no one on my staff will have to spend massive amounts of time and effort to locate, identify, separate, and organize exhibits for the Court.

Preparing our trial exhibit lists is often as simple as copying the tabs from the folders including all those the trial attorney believes are necessary, ignoring those that are not.

Needless to say, you should have a separate folder for each deposition. Depending on the number of pages in the transcript and number of documents attached, perhaps a separate file pocket will be needed. Each folder should contain the notice of deposition, all exhibits, your deposition notes and, of course, the transcript. All in one neat place and accessible at any time.

But no document management system is complete without a comprehensive Cover Sheet (you'll find an example at the end of this chapter).

During the course of handling any file, there is a plethora of communication information you and your staff will use repeatedly, including client file number(s), phone and fax numbers, street and e-mail addresses for the client, other counsel, experts, witnesses, and the Court (including the names of court clerks, bailiffs and court reporters). And if you traveled out of town for your deposition or negotiation, the cover sheet can even contain hotel contact information, especially if you think you will be taking more depositions there or traveling there for meetings. And even though a Cover Sheet for large and complex cases might easily grow to four or five pages, it will greatly simply your life, save piles of time, and eliminate errors.

Obviously, the most important material on the Cover Sheet—your client contact information—goes first, followed by the information for the Court, opposing counsel, other counsel, your experts, etc., on down to the last entry, the least important information, perhaps the phone number of the motel where you stayed in Portland.

Not so many years ago, the information cited above might have been all handwritten and casually stuffed inside a file folder, or scribbled on notes left around the office. This required staff or counsel to scramble each time they needed an address or a phone number, or to scan pages and pages of documentation in search of an opponent's letterhead or marginal scribble amid all the debris.

Thanks to computing, a Cover Sheet is all that's necessary to put the essential information at your fingertips. In fact, it could prove to be the single most helpful element in your document-management system. Without one, the waste of time looking for contact information within in a file is simply unfair to the client, bad for morale, and frustrating for the attorney. And there are some important side benefits to efficiency. It tends to impress clients. A personal example:

Andrew (Andy) Sternwood, a VP for a long-standing client of mine, was appointed to head up the new West Coast office of an international commercial insurance broker. With several assistants and technicians manning the "back room," Sternwood, a charming, well-turned out Brit was the "producer," the salesman. Over several years, I worked with him in relation to claims against his insureds, ranging from oil well blow-outs and cargo damage, to employee parking lot slug-fests. Our results were usually good, perhaps even outstanding by some measures. But Sternwood never seemed very impressed by our efforts, although he was cordial by nature and always pleasant.

Document-management can make a reputation for you and your firm.

Then one day, a British syndicate that underwrote insurance for trucking companies decided to pull the plug. Bad news for the firms insured through Sternwood's brokerage: All 40 had to be given immediate formal notice of a 30-day termination, and the timing couldn't have been worse. Sternwood's second-in-command was out sick, another key staffer was on maternity leave, and the remaining troops had only the barest clue as to how to proceed.

But that's what attorneys are for, so Sternwood called for help.

After asking him to messenger 50 pages of his company's letterhead and envelopes to my office along with the necessary Department of Insurance Notice of Termination forms, and a list of the companies to be notified, with addresses, I drafted a cover letter, filled out a sample form, and turned the matter over to my staff. Later that same afternoon I sent a messenger back to Sternwood's office with a box containing all the completed documents.

"*Brilliant!*" he said in the finest British tradition. "*What a day. We need a whisky or several lagers. Or both. On me! Can you meet me at the Jonathan for drinks at 5?* Having never before been invited to the Jonathan Club—where business royalty meets in Los Angeles—I was happy to comply.

My point? When properly applied, document-management (e.g., organization) not only can save the day, it can also make a reputation for you and your firm.

Sternwood neither understood nor cared about breached insurance contracts, exploding offshore oil platforms, sinking ships, or collapsing construction cranes. He was mostly worried about having all the necessary paperwork to meet a Department of Insurance deadline. And because my document-management system made rapid response possible, I finally made it into the legal pantheon—a man with whom to share a drink at the Jonathan Club.

Depending on memory to find a document is not a system. You need a system.

Right about now, you might be thinking to yourself, *"I don't need a system. I know where everything is!"*

I disagree. You do not know where everything is.

You may recall (approximately) where one piece of paper lies in relation to the rest of the junk on your credenza. And you may remember (approximately) where a document sits in a computer directory in relation to surrounding documents, thus, making it a little easier for you to find. But those are just examples of your mind instinctively trying to impose order on the chaos you have created. That is not a system. You need a system. You *need* a system.

SAMPLE MEMORANDUM

MEMORANDUM

TO: Staff
FROM: R. Priscilla
DATE: November 30, 2012
RE: Cover Sheets

Each of our files should contain a Cover Sheet printed on yellow paper (see sample attached.)

On the first page, the Cover Sheet should include the name of the client and individual to whom we report, including that person's file number, individuals to whom we send copies, and a "Re:" block for the case.

Next should be listed the Court name, address, telephone number, case number, Judge's name, Department/Room number and contacts such as Clerk, Bailiff, Court Reporter.

The top of Page 2 should show the name of primary opposing counsel. Then, other counsel should be listed when, for example, there are multiple parties. Leave at least four lines between entities.

If an insurance matter, the following pages of the Cover Sheet should include the name of our client's insured (with relevant contact names, addresses, telephone, and fax numbers); the names of experts (starting with those we have retained), including addresses, telephone, and fax numbers; the names and the telephone numbers of significant witnesses, or others peripherally involved in the litigation.

The Cover Sheet should be kept on top of the "Correspondence" folder at all times so that when we refer to the file we will have in front of us the names, addresses, telephone numbers, file references and other pertinent information we might require to contact any party or person.

The Cover Sheet should never be placed in the "to be filed" bin. It should be kept always in the Correspondence folder or replaced immediately if removed, for example, for additions, modification or copying.

SAMPLE COVER SHEET

Re: Star Transportation v. Gregor Samsa, Inc.
Crane Collapse - Port of Los Angeles
D/L: 13 October 2012
Our Ref: 0237 12 2217

REPORT TO:
Mr. Ralph Kramden   Rkramden@StarCarriers.com
STAR TRANSPORTATION, INC.
2390 Airport Park Drive
Los Angeles, California 90134
Your ref: LA 06 WP 271
Tel: (800) 277-xxxx Main
(310) 868-xxxx Kramden Direct
(310) 367-xxxx Kramden (Cell)
Fax: (310) 868-xxxx

U.S. District Court - Central District of California
312 North Spring Street
Los Angeles, CA 90010

Hon. Egbert A. Souse, Docket No: CO 765 238
Clerk: William Dunkenfield (213) 206-xxxx
Court Reporter: Amadeo Avogadro (213) 206-xxxx

Walther PPK, Esq., attorney for Gregor Samsa
WALTHER & WESSON
1200 South Figueroa Street
Los Angeles, CA 90016
Tel: (213) 426-xxxx
Fax: (213) 426-xxxx

CHAPTER 7

Finding Real Experts

Experts are a litigation fact of life.

They are born of a requirement of the rules of evidence which informs us that only a "qualified" witness may conclude and testify that the 63-year-old personal injury plaintiff who was working as a janitor at the time he claimed to be injured, would not earn $376 billion over the remainder of his work life, or that the two-person cabinet manufacturing shop with gross revenues averaging $120,000 per year over the first 20 years of its existence, was not realistically valued at $3.7 trillion dollars. Probably not you, and certainly not I, would be permitted to testify to such common-sense conclusions because we are not "experts."

Thus, while an expert is often defined simply as someone who has just a bit more knowledge about a particular field than a person who knows nothing at all, an expert economist or other "credentialed" person is required to testify that a business grossing $100,000 a year cannot, realistically, be expected to be worth more than 10 times that amount at any point in the future. That is, placing a value on the business anywhere over $1 million is simply bad science.

Now, does it take a scientist to tell us this? Not in the real world. But in Court the answer is, "*Yes.*"

There will, on the other hand, arise important (read: major) cases that will require you to have true experts available to determine and describe their findings and conclusions in areas of human endeavor in which neither the jury nor the attorneys at bar have any meaningful knowledge.

Real example:

> Crew members of an offshore supply boat shuttling men and materiel to an oil production platform drink water from a ballast tank instead of the potable water tank because of a malfunctioning switch valve. Although the water is fresh, shore-loaded water, the ballast tank is coated with a rust-retardant we'll call Rust-Away. As a result of the ingestion of the ballast tank water, the crew claims severe injury, including nausea, headache, sleeplessness...and fear of water tanks.

The questions presented included: 1) Is Rust-Away, and any of its ingredients, toxic to any extent? 2) If so, could the toxic elements have leeched into the water in the tank? 3) What were the concentrations of toxic chemicals that leeched into the water, if any? 4) Were those concentrations sufficient to cause the symptoms complained of or, indeed, any symptoms at all?

I had no idea. I needed an expert. Because only an expert toxicologist or industrial chemist would have the expertise required to test the water, isolate its constituent elements, digest the specification data on Rust-Away, and then apply the findings to the known research on the effects to be expected following exposure to those elements in the concentrations found.

So, where do you find a real "expert?"

It is not an idle question because, setting aside Google, the local bar association and its "pay-for-listing" expert directories, and the phone book, most attorneys have no idea where to find a well-qualified orthopedic surgeon, economist, toxicologist, structural engineer, insurance broker or dog trainer. So, they rely on recommendations of friends, other attorneys, or those bar publications which list anyone who cares to pay for the listing. The professional experts may appear to be a good bet at first. But, in my opinion, they are often vulnerable to attack on their credentials and their impartiality. And the more obviously an expert is offering testimony for hire, the more their resume is susceptible to being challenged.

What's the difference between a real expert and a hired gun?

So where do you find a real "expert?"

What I suggest may or may not be obvious, but it works well for me:

When a case requires "real" expertise, look first to one or more of the universities in your area.

The last time I needed a toxicologist on a case I was handling, I called the Department of Chemistry at UCLA, the biggest university campus in my area. I spoke to a professor there, and after describing the issue, he didn't hesitate to refer me to a colleague across town at USC whose research focused on the exact chemicals in the exposure case I was defending. You want "real" experts? Start with the universities. The professors or department chairmen there earn their living doing research and teaching. And while they may accept consultancies and charge for their services, they will give you real information. They are not typical "hired guns."

Most attorneys have no idea how to find well-qualified experts.

Even if you live in Pagosa Springs, Colorado, there is a university a few hours away in Albuquerque, and all you have to do is call. Or, dial the head of the department at Rice University in Houston, Texas, which I did the last time one of my clients in the Far East received $6 million worth of contaminated styrene monomer, and I needed a laboratory to test samples of the product. Within hours after speaking to two professors, I had referrals to two different, highly qualified testing laboratories, one in San Antonio and the other in St. Louis. In fact, for weeks afterward I was receiving calls from other professors, active and retired, who had heard about the request for assistance and had additional advice to offer. For free.

So, finding a real "expert" isn't difficult, provided you know how and where to look.

Further in that regard, I caution you to avoid the expert "mills" that can provide, say, a civil engineer to testify on anything from suspension bridge construction to breakfast food additives.

Once you find your expert, preparing the testimony should be an easy process.

Hopefully, your champion will have testified previously as an expert, and will be familiar with the expectations you will have and the job they are to do. And so much the better if they are familiar with some of the rules of evidence.

Part of your job, of course, is to explain how the process works and how you will be employing that expert. For depositions, you proceed to prepare the expert much as you would an ordinary fact witness. That means providing the witness Lifeline which, as noted earlier, must be made available to every witness to allow them to defend themselves by bringing the discussion back to the point they want to make. Your expert may have to admit that the "explosion" would not have occurred had your client's employee not lit a cigarette in a non-smoking area. But before making that admission, he can also point out the direct cause of the explosion was the natural gas leak (the gas company's fault), or the insufficiency of signs warning of the hazard (the landowner's fault).

Finding a real expert isn't difficult, but avoid the expert "mills".

What's the difference between a real expert and a "hired gun?"

A real expert bases opinions on solid research and real science, not just "*30 years of experience working on geothermal projects, Sonny.*" And it follows that the better credentialed the expert, the less they are likely to become defensive and flustered under careful examination. Indeed, when I am examining a "hired gun" consultant, I generally find some way to express my skepticism at their credentials, methodology, or conclusions, so as to goad them into losing emotional control.

In one deposition, I had an expert trapped into admitting a number of exaggerations in his resume and, finally, he blurted out, "*You're a miserable bastard, you know that?*" Me? A hard-working, law-abiding officer of the Court, born within the hallowed state of holy matrimony, and seeking only to further the cause of truth and justice, is slanderously attacked by an expert witness. That response is exactly the type that opposing counsel does not want on the record.

> "*So, Mr. Expert, what is it about the simple, entirely proper questions I was asking that made you so angry? What was so wrong about asking if you had read the leading treatise in the field in which you claim to be expert?*"

That case settled, of course, as I seriously doubt opposing counsel could have risked putting that expert on the stand knowing I would eventually get around to "the" question. Because if the answer at trial was anything other than a repeat of, "*You're a miserable bastard...*" a lot of explanation would have been required.

Still, real experts may require some work as far as their testimony is concerned because they spend most of their time in a research laboratory at the university rather than testifying in various courtrooms or giving depositions. But that is exactly why they will help your case. Any jury and any judge will be able to recognize real expertise. Incidentally, a little bit of arrogance is acceptable in an expert; too much humility leads to equivocation and weakens the presentation. Physicians are usually convincing experts because they tend to believe they are among The Chosen. Their work requires self-confidence and self-esteem that, on occasion, borders on arrogance.

You want an expert that the jury wants to believe for reasons beyond the resume.

Some other qualities you need to take into account:

- You must be certain that your expert can testify with conviction. They should have a quiet confidence, but without the bluff and bluster of the "testimony-for-hire" types.
- You want an expert with a clear and pleasant speaking voice. Professors are accustomed to public speaking in class and at symposia and other professional events, so they usually have that quality. But not all do. A thin, squeaky voice or a quirky speaking style laced with "*ers,*" "*ums,*" and "*maybes,*" is not going to help your case.
- You want to select an expert that the jury will want to believe for reasons beyond the resume. If, on some rare occasion, you have reason to retain the world's leading authority in any given field, the overwhelmingly impressive credentials will trump an unpolished speaking style. But that is very rare. You will need a blend of true expertise and professional, polished style to carry the day.

That said, you certainly can work with the expert to develop and improve presentation skills, but you don't want to spend an inordinate amount of time doing so. Nor will your expert want to take that time. So use your initial contacts, often by telephone or perhaps an interview at the expert's office, where you can also use environmental cues to gauge the person's character and predilections, to determine if this is the person who can do the job you require.

CHAPTER 8

Liability & Damages

For every human endeavor with any kind of goal, you must be able to isolate and analyze the two or three most important factors affecting your strategy, tactics, and actions. The two most important factors for a skydiver might be *chute integrity* and *weather*. For a physician, it might be *diagnosis* and *vital signs*.

For a lawyer evaluating a case, the two most important factors come down to *liability* and *damages*. For that reason, this chapter may be the most important in my crash course for litigators.

Case evaluation crystallizes the focus of every trial lawyer's existence. It's all that matters in any civil case you will ever handle. And every significant report to your client should include an assessment of liability and damages --or at the least—a discussion of how the events being reported affect liability and damages.

Your earliest reports—and subsequent reports describing the discovery of meaningful information, deposition testimony, or judicial proceedings—should contain detailed analysis. But always remember, you should base your recommendations, and expect your client to base his or her authority whether to accept a settlement offer, pay a settlement demand, or proceed to trial, on your analysis of liability and damages. *That is what you do, so you might as well realize it, internalize it, and set out to do it well.* Whether there are numerous, equally weighted variables—or one or two that overwhelm the scales—you are only trying to calculate in two dimensions: liability and damages.

In case evaluation, there are two primary factors: liability and damages.

As a plaintiff's lawyer, your analysis will inform you whether or not to take the case, how much you believe the case is worth, and what are the probabilities for success (calculated with as much mathematical certainty as possible). As defense counsel, you are also interested in what the case may be worth, whether a jury is likely to decide for plaintiff or your client, and what—in view of the potential risks and rewards—would be a reasonable settlement.

Often, the analysis of liability is simple and obvious.

- In an automobile accident involving a rear-end collision, the car struck from the rear is going to win. Liability will be assessed against the following car even if the car in front stopped short. The following car should have left enough distance to stop in an emergency.
- The owner of the cargo dumped overboard by the negligent vessel operators will collect damages from the ocean carrier even if the cargo was poorly packed.

In most cases, however (and this includes almost all corporate litigation), the facts and evidence and legal precedents, and the testimony of various witnesses, may all be so vague, contradictory, and convoluted, that—more than any other factors—the ultimate finding of liability will depend on the artistry of the lawyer and the like-ability of the witnesses.

I have handled cases—large offshore oil production platform explosions, for example—where there were dozens of eyewitnesses and numerous experts with accounts and opinions of what happened. In my experience, it is extremely rare for one witness, or even one expert, to be able to piece together exactly what may have occurred. Which makes perfect sense, because each witness, percipient or expert, has a perspective, a subjective view, that impacts that witness' perception and often interferes with his recollection. For example, in an offshore explosion, you would expect a witness on the platform to be terrified while a witness on a supply vessel half a mile away would not have panic interfering with their vision or coloring their recollection.

Psychologists tell us the "subjective being" creates and shapes the observation itself. In my world, I'm aware of three types of snow—heavy and wet, icy and hard, light and fluffy. Toward the Arctic Circle, though, the *Inuit* people have more than 35 words for snow. They actually distinguish different forms of snow that I cannot. Some witnesses have three words for explosion and others have ten.

In reaching a conclusion, and preparing the story about liability, an attorney must be able to tease apart all the subjectivity, and weave the threads into a coherent whole that will be presented to the jury as objective truth.

I have tried cases where I was convinced my story was the truth; that it was the only way to fit all the testimony and all the evidence into a seamless whole. Sometimes one or more witnesses had the same picture. Often, no one witness could connect all the dots. On some occasions, I could not connect the dots either, and I believe no one will ever know exactly what actually happened down to the last detail. Of course, the opposition is also trying to determine the "real" story, and present it to the trier of fact. That's why we have juries: To vote on which story they like best or, increasingly, which party and which attorney they like best.

Clearly, if no possible defendant has any conceivable liability, or plaintiff's damages are so small as to be non-existent, no plaintiff's counsel would be interested in taking that case.

On the other hand, if defense counsel realizes there is no possible defense to liability, no mitigating factors, no possible excuse or explanation, and damages are measurable only by the largest networked computers, then any amount that plaintiffs demand that is close to reasonable must be paid. At least your client will save the cost of your legal fees, an expense which must always be considered when calculating potential exposure to damages.

Fortunately, only rarely is life or the law so clear-cut.

There are always mitigating factors to support a defense.

There are always mitigating factors to support a defense, even a feeble one. There are always ways to interpret financial data to attempt to show the loss is not as large as might first be assumed. Note that in certain cases, damages may be fixed to a fair degree of certainty.

Consider a cargo case:

> A container improperly stacked and left unsecured goes overboard during ocean transit. You have commercial invoices, packing lists, bills of lading, and dozens of other documents that establish the nature and value of the lost goods. Of course, there may be some haggling over freight charges, adjuster's fees, interest, and court costs. But if the goods were valued at $100,000 on the commercial invoice, for example, you'll

be on pretty firm ground telling your client that's about what the case is worth, setting aside any viable contractual or legal limitations.

On the other hand, in a business dispute or personal injury claim, damages can be very slippery, and assessing them more art than science. As we saw in Chapter 3 (deposition technique), the value of the claim of the injured seaman might vary widely depending on whether a jury can be persuaded that all or some significant part of plaintiff's post-accident problems, physical or psychological, pre-existed the event. To the extent it can be estimated, the end result might only be the difference between an award of $3 million or $4 million, but, needless to say, plaintiffs would rather have the *four* and defendants would rather pay the *three*.

Similarly, in a business dispute, you will have dueling economists and business evaluators setting the value of the disputed behavior in a range, let's say, from $10 million to $100 million. It is the job of the competent attorney to analyze the factors that account for the disparate estimates. That requires the attorney to determine, among other variables, which positions of which "experts" will be most persuasive to a jury; indeed, which experts themselves will be most appealing to a jury, and which theories, standards, data, and economic models the attorney herself feels she will be most able to sell to a jury while defending against opposing theories.

The finding of liability often depends on witness like-ability and the lawyer's artistry.

It is important to be honest with yourself in your appraisal.

Many attorneys manage to convince themselves of a legal position certain their confidence alone will carry the day. If they fail to evaluate their position realistically, though, those are the attorneys who get hit. And by getting *hit*, I do not mean losing. If you win a lot less money than you should have won, or you lose a lot more than you should have lost, you've been *hit*. If your client gets life when you suggested the most he would get is three-to-five, or if you're a D.A. seeking life without possibility of parole and the jury gives the defendant six months, you've been *hit*.

A $10 million loss is acceptable, and a client will even be somewhat grateful for that result, if your analysis reveals they should have lost $20 million and you have clearly and completely explained why. Incidentally, you should understand that cases are tried because of unrealistic expectations on one side or the other or both. In a case where you conclude your client is likely to lose between $15 million and $20 million, you should be willing to settle for any figure below $15 million. If the lowest demand the other side makes is $50 million, however, you have little choice but to proceed to trial. Any jury verdict up to $50 million saves your client money, but common sense dictates you want a result less than $25 million to support your analysis. Being *hit* in these circumstances would mean losing more than $25 million or so.

Of course, if you lose $100 million, you've been more than hit... you've been *obliterated.*

One case I use for training purposes was reported prominently in a periodical devoted to analysis of *quanta,* the amounts juries award:

> Merchant seaman slips in shower and injures knee. Plaintiff demands $75,000. Defendants offer $15,000. The jury awards $1,750,000. Someone's analysis was way off.

For plaintiffs, the results work the other way around.

You believe the case is worth $50 million at a minimum, and so advise your client. Defendants offer $20 million, which you reject. You proceed to trial and win $10 million. *You've been hit.* You could have settled for double what you ultimately obtained at trial. You left $10 million on the table, even though you "won."

Needless to say, there are numerous subcategories of considerations.

For example, a prudent attorney should be aware that he is more likely to effectively "sell" an economic model to a jury if the model was developed at Harvard, tested and respected worldwide, and praised in every economic text published since 1802, compared to a competing model that was developed by the attorney's kid sister as her first statistics class project. That is not to say the kid sister's model is not every bit as good as the Harvard model and, in fact, it's brilliance and clarity may ultimately win universal acceptance. But a jury is more likely to go with the Harvard model, and counsel must recognize this reality even if he deplores the result the Harvard model yields and fervently believes in his sister's work. Counsel's duty is to report the LIKELY result to her client, even if that result does not favor the client.

Which leads to a very important consideration:

When do you give the client the bad news? When do you let a client know getting out of the morass is going to cost money, or, for plaintiffs, yield much less than they want? You could say, "*As soon as I'm sure of that result and how much it will cost.*" But that would be an evasion. No attorney can ever be 100 percent certain of a liability result nor of a finding of quanta, the amount of damages a jury will award. But the sooner the attorney can gather sufficient information and documentation to reasonably estimate a figure, and the sooner this figure is transmitted to the client, the better.

Bad news is not dessert; it should never be saved for last.

I have seen cases where, based on little more than wishful thinking, defense counsel advises the client that the lawsuit can be settled for a low-ball figure; say, $30,000. After some discovery, preliminary settlement talks, a little Motion practice, a lot of billing—and a whole lot of huffing and puffing—counsel reports to client that $30,000-to-$50,000 will "make the problem disappear." Then, six weeks before trial, counsel advises the corporate client if it doesn't come up with at least $300,000, the case will proceed to trial, and the judgment in favor of plaintiff will likely be at least $500,000!

I know how this case was handled and reported because, six weeks before trial, the file was pulled from counsel and turned over to my office. The sad part was, when that defense counsel finally got around to doing his job, carefully evaluating the facts and the law, his conclusions were pretty sound. The case was indeed worth $300,000, and we ultimately settled, one week before trial, for $220,000. How frustrating it must have been for that attorney to have lost the file and lost his client after doing such good work. My advice to that attorney, however, and my advice to you is this:

Do your good work sooner, not later. And report it to your client immediately.

Start your analysis as soon as possible, and report to your client every step of the way. Don't be afraid to second-guess yourself.

As soon as an experienced attorney picks up a file and reads through the documents the first time, she gets a feel for the ultimate result. She begins to imagine what she will want a certain witness to say. She will notice documentation that is missing or incomplete, and she will imagine what she wants those documents to reveal. If she is not intimately familiar with every aspect of the controlling law, or all precedent addressing the vital issues, she will imagine what she wants those cases to say. Part of her job as an advocate is to discover, explain, reveal, and bring forth those elements she can imagine will help her case and crush her opposition.

You can report the best-case scenario to the client, but only as a hypothetical. You must temper your vision with a healthy dose of caution and understanding that reality may not be everything you have on your wish list. After all, witnesses may not say what you hoped they would say; the documents may not reveal what you hoped they would reveal, and—as is often the case—the law may turn out to be lot more vague and a lot less settled than you ever imagined, if not directly against your position.

Damage estimates are more art than science.

You must report this to the client as well.

As to reporting legal conclusions, it's probably better not to report anything until at least preliminary research has been undertaken and a feel has been gained for where the ultimate result will lie. You can report, preliminarily, that the law seems to be on the client's side or not, but that further lines of research remain to be explored. Of course, it is often the case that counsel will generally know the law in a specific area and is relatively certain what result will be obtained. That should be reported early, especially if it is not a happy picture for the client.

Grayson's Rule: *Bad news is not dessert; it should never be saved for last!* In the case just described, the first report to the client should have warned that a judgment against the client as high as $500,000 might be in the offing. If counsel was clearly convinced that settlement could be accomplished for $30,000, she might have offered something along the lines of, "*Despite this high exposure, however, it may be possible to achieve settlement in the mid-five-figure range.*" Instead, as is clear, counsel did no homework, and undertook no meaningful research or analysis until very shortly before trial.

There are two lessons to be learned here:

Lesson #1

Do your analysis as soon as you can. You may not have all the facts or documents, but you do not have to know everything to a certainty to write a coherent report. You can estimate how the results in the case may be affected by what the facts and documents ultimately reveal. But you must be clear about what you *don't* know, and then be diligent about finding it. Most important, the law will be available for you to research from the very outset, and you can suggest to the client how the law will be applied depending on what facts ultimately come to light.

Lesson #2

Don't go out on any limbs until you are certain you have enough facts, evidence, and law beneath you to soften a fall. You have a duty to make a call for your client, but do so with a statement of what you know and what remains to be learned. If it is ever necessary to change your evaluation of liability or damages, you will have no problem so long as the revision is mandated by newly discovered facts or evidence. You must not, however, raise an evaluation of exposure and settlement potential from $30,000 to $300,000 simply because trial is drawing near, and you finally do the analysis which informs that the earlier figure was based on wishful thinking and not reality.

Don't go out on a limb until you have enough facts under you to soften a fall.

And the corollary rule: Never go so far out on a limb that there is no alternative to jumping without a parachute.

There is no reason to paint yourself into a corner, even if you are relatively certain it is safe. And you should never do so in the early stages of a case. You simply do not know enough to predict an outcome, even if your vast experience suggests you can handle this one with your eyes shut. Don't try it. Something in the facts, one of the witnesses, a recently discovered document, an e-mail written by an incompetent assistant; something may be out there you do not yet see, and perhaps can't even imagine will upset your universe. So, leave the door open to modification.

If disaster—large or small—does strike, you simply report it to your client, along with your reminder that one of those uncontrollable variables—say, a pending Appellate Court ruling now in the books—has tilted the picture. These are the things you have prepared your client to accept, and which, now in existence, require you and your client to reconsider your position.

Interestingly, if you estimate high to start—$500,000 as opposed to $30,000—you are more likely to find that the "unknown" litigation elements—unforeseen factors that almost always appear in litigation—will favor your client more often than they will hurt. Much better to estimate the high figure, and to be able to report a final settlement at less than 50 percent of that figure than to estimate low and then start screaming for 10 times that amount as Armageddon approaches. For one thing, you'll keep more clients; for another, your clients will trust you because you give them all the news, good and bad, as you learn it, analyze it, and report it as it affects them.

A slick hustler might think, *"I'll just tell every defendant they might lose $6 billion and be a hero when I settle it out for $1 million."* Or plaintiff's counsel might think, *"I'll mention this case may be worth $50,000, and won't my client be amazed and grateful when I get them $225,000?"*

You cannot "trick" the analysis.

If, as plaintiff, you grossly underestimate value, you just might find your clients leaving you, seeking out less timid hustlers who happily promise a settlement in the millions of dollars and then deliver only thousands. Of course, that's not your problem, any more than the malpractice suit they file against that other attorney.

But you shouldn't let it go that far.

You should have some basis for suggesting value that is close to reasonable so that you will not be the one looking at the malpractice suit. Of course, experience is a great teacher here, and a "feel" for case value will come with handling a lot of cases. But only if there has been proper evaluation, complete gathering and analysis of the facts, and a comprehensive review of the applicable law.

Know the important questions and dedicate yourself to finding the answers.

Similarly, defendants—corporations, insurance companies, and most individuals—are not naive. They know every lawsuit won't expose them to multi-million dollar judgments, and they will question the ability and analytical power of an attorney who grossly overestimates every lawsuit.

Your analysis must be thorough and reasonable, capable of clear explanation, and informative on open questions that will affect the analysis of liability and calculation of damages when they become known.

Clients will be confident in you *not* because you claim to know all the answers, but because you appear to know the important questions and are dedicated to finding the answers. You should also educate your clients to the fact this is what you do to protect them. You do not make wild predictions that they might find pleasing but which have little relation to reality. You prepare them with the truth of their situation to the extent it can be determined.

There is no set rule as to when you should begin to consolidate your analysis and stake out positions. Like the story of Goldilocks and The Three Bears, the porridge has to be just right. The attorney who taught me a lot of what I know about practicing law—a learned, ethical, and very thoughtful man—used to drive me crazy when he would critique my early reports to clients.

To a large extent, the verdict will be based on you.

"*Mahhhtin*" he would say in his Southern drawl, "*You can't go tellin' this client what this case is going to be worth until you have more information. Do you know what the evidence is going to be? Do you know how strong the other side's witnesses are? Have you researched all the law in this area and believe you know what an appellate court will do? Why don't you just make some suggestions here, describe what's happening now, and what we still have to look at before you start drawing lines in the sand?*"

Thus chastened, I would slink back to my desk, make the necessary changes, add more analysis (always more analysis), and inform the client that we would continue to keep them advised of all significant events and findings.

A few weeks later I might be in my boss's office again with a carefully worded, cautiously pessimistic, and fairly non-committal report, sitting on the desk between us.

"*Mahhhtin,*" he would say with great patience, "*You are an attorney, not a research assistant. You are here to advise your clients, to help them. You have to make them fully aware of all aspects of the litigation, all the issues and all the contingencies, of course. But you still have to make the call. You have to put it on the line and, to the best of your ability, let them know what's going to happen and why and how, and exactly what we're going to do about it.*"

And then he would smile. "*Or try to do about it.*"

To this day, I am convinced the only thing that kept me from flying across that desk and throttling him where he sat was the fact that he was a solid 6'-4" and could have pounded me into a veal cutlet without disturbing his water carafe. He drove me nuts. But he taught me that important lesson. It's more art than science how and when you start making the calls, and it all starts with the analysis. In many cases, the analysis itself will inform you when it is ready to be revealed. It speaks clearly, it does not have many gaps, or at least none that aren't recognized and explained, and it has begun to form itself into the narrative that will be the story you are going to tell at trial, the magic you are going to weave for the jury.

Before then, it's just a pile of data and speculation, eligible for discussion, but not ripe for conclusion.

As an aside, legal research works much the same way. It begins to form itself and take on a shape as you wade through it, organize it, and prioritize your findings. And it will tell you when you've completed the task. My own rule is to wait until I run into the same leading case from at least three different sources, whether they are reported cases, treatises, annotations, encyclopedias, colleagues, or prayer. By the time I'm spinning around and chasing my tail but not coming up with any new cases or any new discussion, I know it's time to move on to another issue.

Now, about calculating damages:

There are at least two exercises you must always employ in your calculations.

First, use forms and formulae.

Second, use your opponent's check-list and plug in your own numbers.

Forms and formulae are tools you can learn from experienced seniors and form books. For example, for personal injury cases you must calculate pecuniary damages including lost wages and benefits, past and future medical expenses, cost of replacement or repair of property lost or damaged, and other items on which a more or less definite value can be placed. General damages include pain and suffering, loss of society, enjoyment of life, and other items which are left to the discretion of the jury as there is no way to set a mathematical value on such losses. As a rule, however, defense counsel can use a multiple of pecuniary damages to estimate general damages. So, if lost wages and medical expenses for a 25-year-old burn victim who will never work again total $2 million, one can assume a jury will award between $6 and $10 million dollars in general damages. The more horrific the injury or death the higher the multiple.

These figures will be modified by liability, of course, although that is not supposed to be how a jury operates.

A jury is supposed to make a finding on liability and a finding on damages, and then the judge apportions the money. That is, a jury may find the plaintiff 50 percent at fault for his own injuries because, after all, he was his toking on his own crack pipe and that action triggered the explosion. There are lots of 'No Smoking" signs on offshore oil platforms and crack use is generally frowned upon anywhere, so this may not be the most sympathetic plaintiff a jury will ever encounter. While juries almost always decide a badly injured worker should "get something," they often make smaller awards to plaintiffs they don't like very much, even though the judge will instruct them not to give such matters any thought.

All of these rules of thumb, along with the application of mitigating factors, must be considered when analyzing potential damages. And reporting the analysis to the client should be realistic.

You may have strong evidence that plaintiff was smoking crack but you may not be able to get that evidence before the jury which, as a result, may have an entirely sympathetic view of the injured man. And you don't want to tell your client that you can blow plaintiff out of the water with your evidence of crack use when all the jury may get to hear at trial is that he *might* have started the fire when he lit up a Marlboro by mistake, being groggy after striking his head on an overhead valve and forgetting where he was for a minute, having worked 36 hours straight without food. You just never know what a witness is going to "remember" at the last minute.

In business cases, the calculation of damages may be heavily dependent on your expert's analysis. That is, in casualty cases, where property is damaged, the calculation is driven by documents such as invoices, receipts, repair quotations and the like, documents which you can use to reach fairly accurate conclusions about the amount of the loss. For corporate claims, however, an economist will probably be needed to analyze profit and loss, the value of good will, and other factors which are the domain of accountants and actuaries and, of course, plaintiffs' imaginations.

The second point, using your opponent's checklist, is rather straightforward.

You must consider not what you believe damages should be—or even what you believe the jury will determine them to be—but what your opponent believes they should be and, more importantly, *why* she believes in her calculation. You must try to learn the elements of her calculation through discovery and then assign value to those elements. For personal injury cases, this is rather simple. Use the total of pecuniary damages and multiply by 10. Remember, if you have included all elements of loss and assigned reasonable values, the five-times pecuniary damages factor should approximate actual case value or exposure. Plaintiff's wish list, however, often contains at least a ten-times factor.

BACK STORY

After a hearing on motions, I once settled an oil field personal injury case in a courthouse cafeteria in a small town in central California.

At the time, I was having coffee before the long drive back to Los Angeles. Just then, opposing counsel showed up, and we started talking settlement. At one point, he said his client's case was worth at least $650,000. I laughed, and I showed him a report to my client—dated three months earlier—predicting plaintiff's settlement demand. My guess: $600,000. I was just off by $50,000, and counsel was shocked that I was able to predict his demand so accurately. The case settled soon after for $100,000, far below its true value because I'm convinced that counsel thought I either had super powers of perception...or that I had bugged his office. Nothing of the sort.

My only trick was to do counsel's homework from *his* perspective.

Because he was a competent, if a bit inexperienced, I had a pretty good idea how he would approach his evaluation. So I just added together all the elements of pecuniary loss that could be obtained from medical billing records and plaintiff's employment history, multiplied by a factor of 10—and then assumed that plaintiff would be a bit more generous with himself than I—and came up with $600,000. That this conclusion was in my report three months before counsel and I met over coffee in the courthouse cafeteria probably convinced him I had bugged his office and heard him tell his client something like, "*Anything around $100,000 would be a good result.*" Even though I knew of no such statement, and even though counsel was probably expecting to settle for a great deal more, he was so shaken by having his strategy predicted months in advance, he lost his will to carry on.

CHAPTER 9

Thinking on Your Feet

Now and then, everyone is capable of delivering the perfect retort to a tough or embarrassing question. But let's face it, some are just more facile than others.

Nature aside, though, there is something every trial lawyer can do to present themselves as a lightning-fast thinker. It's a variation of the Lifeline technique introduced in Chapter 4.

Here's how it works:

Suppose you're appearing in Bankruptcy Court, where you seldom venture. You seek to have the Judge set aside the automatic stay that protects debtors who have filed for bankruptcy protection so you can pursue discovery, and prosecute a claim against the debtor to the extent it has insurance to cover the loss. You have done your research, and you know you are on firm legal ground. Liability (as opposed to property) insurance is not an asset of the debtor's estate, but is expressly for the protection of third parties—your clients—who have suffered a loss for which it is clear the debtor's insurance will likely provide indemnity. You are presenting your arguments and legal authority in your usual fluid (dare we say, spell-binding) manner when the Judge suddenly interrupts.

"*Well, what about the ruling in Wizard v. Oz?*" he says.

Wizard v. Oz?

You know you had heard of it, but you thought it was a Kansas State Court case involving a lost dog. What to do? Think on your feet, of course. Even though the only thing your feet are telling you is…"RUN!"

Suddenly, you remember the Lifeline you rehearsed for just such an occasion.

"Your Honor," you say, barely skipping a beat, *"I must admit I had thought Wizard was inapplicable to the case at hand. But, may it please the Court, I will revisit Wizard immediately following the hearing and ask only the Court's indulgence to file a supplemental brief to address the additional issues."*

You might also ask the Court for the particular holding in Wizard that should be addressed, or perhaps request a continuance of the hearing for a brief period.

Either way, the crisis will have been averted, and others in the court—probably the judge, too—will be thinking, *"Now, there's an attorney who can think on his feet."*

Do not be surprised if, at some later point in the hearing, having been counseled by his law clerk or having had a moment of legal insight, the Judge mentions his earlier reference to Wizard, and notes that maybe Wizard dealt with peripheral questions and need not be considered after all. I've seen it happen. Even if it does not, however, you will have made the best of a bad situation with grace and competence.

There is another response that qualifies as "thinking on your feet." It's an extension of a judo technique to be discussed in the next chapter.

For now, the advice is just this:

When pushed, yield the ground. Simply apologize. Admit you did not encounter Wizard in your research, and ask if the Court would be so kind as to instruct why Wizard has bearing on the matter at hand. *"Your Honor, I'm embarrassed to have missed the relevant authority, but I would appreciate your advice, and ask that you not punish my client for an error I alone committed."* These are the words of an attorney who thinks on their feet no matter how many times the words have been rehearsed.

CHAPTER 10

Getting the Court on Your Side

Lawyering by its nature encourages aggression, and many lawyers consider courtesy, dignity, and humility to be character flaws.

But understanding how these same traits can also be important tools is helpful in disarming the opposition, and persuading judges that you are on the side of truth and justice, thus speeding you toward your goal. This is especially true when it concerns words coming from the bench. You should treat them as holy writ, no less significant than God's pronouncements to Moses. Because on that day, in that courtroom, at that moment, that judge IS the law.

Thus, my advice to you is simple: When you go before the throne, do not be negative.

Anything the judge suggests is a good idea, even if it means your Motion—a Motion that would be summarily granted in 99.997 percent of all courtrooms in all jurisdictions on the planet—will be denied. Give it up. The judge has spoken. No matter how absurd the Court's pronouncements, greet them as though even Solomon and Einstein working together could not have hoped to achieve such wisdom and insight.

Of course, that doesn't mean you shrivel up and blow away.

After responding so prudently and signaling to the judge and opposing counsel that you are a reasonable, cooperative, thoroughly professional and courteous attorney, you can use the ground you have just gained to wring concessions from the Court or counsel. You might even obtain the result you desired in the first place if not the ruling on the record.

Example:

> Your client is a Japanese corporation, and its president resides in Tokyo. You have filed suit on behalf of the company in Los Angeles because that is where the defendant corporation is domiciled. Mr. President's deposition has been noticed for Tokyo. He doesn't want to be deposed at all; certainly not in Tokyo, where he will have to suffer the humiliation and diminished stature resulting from being summoned to answer questions by a foreign attorney, and then return to the office to face the unspoken questions and pitying glances of colleagues and staff. You have explained to your client the function of the Federal Rules of Civil Procedure, and that the only alternative to participating in discovery is to dismiss the lawsuit. Opposing counsel has brought a Motion to Compel and you have opposed on assorted, losing, theories. Now, at hearing, it is clear the judge is prepared to rule in favor of the moving party and, indeed, may already have issued a tentative ruling ordering the deposition forward.

Do not argue the Motion.

You know your opposition is a loser—and the judge may have even signaled you are going to lose—even if you believe you crafted terribly clever arguments. While you might allude to your arguments, noting that the President is unlikely to have any information of import to the case at hand, you concede that the deposition should and will go forward.

> "*May it please the Court,*" you might say. "*Might the deposition go forward at a time and place which would reduce the expense and inconvenience for all involved? As much as an all-expense paid trip to Tokyo would be enjoyable, wouldn't the excessive cost be best saved against a possible settlement? In the meantime, as Mr. President is about to plan a trip to Los Angeles, would the Court not deem it reasonable to rule that the deposition go forward right here in this jurisdiction, where Court-approved interpreters are available and court reporters would not have to fly half-way around the world? Indeed, where counsel could be comfortable in his own conference room?*"

Even though you have conceded the Motion being granted, you have given the Court more than adequate reason to prohibit the free travel extravaganza to Tokyo that you imply is at the heart of opposing counsel's Motion. You have given the Court a chance to be fair, even-handed, and economically prudent. You may have lost the Motion but you have won the day, walking off with the result that you and your client desired.

Granted, not all situations might be so easy to sway in your favor.

Some Motions are simply win or lose. But often the opportunity is available to obtain at least a portion of your goal, even if it is just an extension of time that would make your client comfortable, but is beyond the urgent deadline sought by the opposition. Specious arguments will lose you the respect of the Court at that moment, and for the entire length of the case. Even a too-vigorous argument to a judge who has already decided to rule against you will lose you some points in the "good guy" sweepstakes, and destroy the possibility of getting any concessions. Know when to back up gracefully, and grab any crumbs that might be available even though you would have preferred the whole sandwich.

Specious arguments will lose you the respect of the Court for the length of the case.

In short, concede...and conquer.

The same tactic can be used in straight negotiations with opposing counsel but must be subtle.

Like many attorneys, I am offended if opposing counsel, when asked for a courtesy—like moving a deposition date back a few weeks or granting an extension for response to discovery—immediately adds conditions such as, "*You can have an extra 10 days but you must waive all objections,*" or, "*We can move the deposition but you have to pay for the original transcript.*" I always reject such proposals, advising counsel that I will, if necessary, simply answer discovery requests immediately, interposing appropriate objections, and will supplement responses as required when further information or documentation becomes available.

For a deposition, I advise that I will simply write a letter formally requesting the continuance of opposing counsel. If it isn't granted without conditions, I will require counsel to go to the trouble and expense of bringing a Motion to Compel the deposition on the original date, a Motion which counsel knows the Court will not grant as we are willing to make the witness available without objection after the requested delay. Unless the suggested deposition date pushes right into the start of trial, there are few, if any, judges who will not grant a short continuance. The point to make to counsel is that you are asking for the courtesy seeking to avoid gamesmanship. But if necessary, you will play any game required.

On the other hand, the way to advance your own cause in such situations is obvious, assuming you are the attorney being asked for an extension or continuance. Rather than seeking a *quid pro quo*, agree to the request...no hesitation, no conditions. Just be a good guy or gal. You should, of course, point out that you're happy to assist opposing counsel as you are certain they will reciprocate if and when requested.

If you want opposing counsel to cooperate with you, strike a collegial note.

It might go something like this:

> *"...At the early meeting under Federal Rule 26, counsel mentioned there were photographs of a discharge survey available somewhere in the file. A copy of those photos might help us all isolate the damages and move us toward an early resolution. Can you send over a set? We'll be happy to reimburse copy costs."*

You can, of course, obtain the photos by propounding formal discovery. But you can save a lot of effort and expense by getting counsel to cooperate with you. And the way to do that is to concede the easy ones and strike a collegial note.

Earlier, I mentioned a case in which opposing counsel was a biker-turned-attorney who still lived by the law of the streets and occasionally found himself suspended by the Bar for playing loose with the rules.

Although he was initially suspicious when I treated him like a full member of the legal community in good standing, counsel responded by becoming fairly easy to work with, setting aside the aggressive, argumentative, non-cooperating, self-pitying, defensive, and hostile personality he exhibited at our first encounter. In that case, simply ceding respect to one unaccustomed to receiving it (without considering whether he deserved it or not) was sufficient to move the contest out of the arena of unrelenting hostility to one of rather cordial competition. The result for my client was a meaningful savings in time and expense as well as a very reasonable settlement at the end of the day. The benefit to me—beyond the good result for my client—was a year with much less stress, aggravation, and tension than might have been the case.

As I mentioned at the outset, lawyering by its nature encourages aggression. While courtesy, dignity, and humility are often seen to be character flaws, I hope I've shown that these traits—seen in their true perspective and used effectively—can help disarm the opposition and speed you toward your goal. Sometimes conceding easy points helps you reach your goal even if it appears you "lost" the argument.

CHAPTER 11

Reporting to Clients

I met Larry K during my senior year of law school. I was interviewing for a job at a San Francisco law firm, and Larry was a partner at that firm. I ended up staying in New Orleans, but Larry and I stayed in touch, and a few years later he showed up in New Orleans as VP-General Counsel for a big steamship line. Over drinks one evening, I asked him, now that he was on the "client" side, what he would do differently if he ever went back to the role of outside counsel.

Without hesitation, he said, "*I would report to the client a lot more often than I did when I was with the firm.*"

So, that's an easy first tip: Report more often.

And I would add, *report more coherently.*

In more than 25 years of practice, I have seen a lot of client "reports" using too many words to say too little. Yes, there are times to be explicit and times to be non-committal—even some rare times when you want to pick up the phone instead of putting a concern in writing. But it generally helps the lawyer/client relationship, and the progress of the litigation, if you let your client know you have something meaningful to say and then say it clearly.

This rule applies to litigation as well as any transactional work.

There are always "issues" that need to be handled, and the purpose of your report should always be to define and analyze those issues, and to offer your conclusions and recommendations as appropriate. Note: An abbreviated *Report to Client* is located at the end of this chapter to show a template of a comprehensive report. A more complete sample is available in the Appendix.

Here's an example of one client report. What do you make of it?

To: Joe Claims Adjuster
XYZ Insurance Company
Re: ABC Shipping Co. Ref: 20288
Vessel Collision/Fatalities

Dear Mr. Adjuster:

We write to bring you up to date with respect to the status of the above-referenced matter. As previously reported, our Motion for Judgment on the Pleadings regarding the claims of Plaintiffs was continued. The Motion will now be heard on October 12. Since our last report, we have also had an opportunity to meet with counsel for the lead plaintiffs (Curley and Moe). We summarize the results of our recent efforts below: We met with Curley and Moe, counsel for the lead plaintiffs. As you know, at this time, XYZ Shipping and S.S. Steamship (the Captain's employer) are the only remaining defendants. Our discussions focused on the strategy to employ in mediation as well as a trial strategy should any party fail to meaningfully participate in settlement discussions.

With respect to the latter proposition, our discussions were focused on limiting XYZ's exposure at time of trial to the policy limits. Plaintiffs were receptive to a proposition that would leave XYZ in the case for purposes of trial. It seems Plaintiffs view it as a great benefit to have XYZ at trial also arguing that S.S. should face substantial responsibility given the captain's operation of the vessel on the day of the accident. We anticipate any agreement reached with the plaintiffs will require that XYZ meaningfully defend the case including the retention of certain experts. We would anticipate such experts would be focused on issues of the toxic fume release and navigation of the vessel with the testimony centered on the captain's actions both before and during the fateful voyage.

We are continuing our negotiations with the plaintiffs and hope to have a written proposal regarding a settlement that would involve our participation at trial for consideration in the near future.

We will continue to keep you up to date with respect to all developments in this matter including our efforts outlined above. In the interim, as always, should you have any questions or comments regarding the above or the matter in general, please feel free to contact us.

Very truly yours.

This is a slightly edited version of an actual client report prepared by an experienced senior associate. Many client reports are about this quality; some better, some worse. In my opinion, it contains vague double-speak without real analysis, and makes only oblique reference to matters of substance.

Let's look at it point by point:

a. *"Our discussions focused on the strategy to employ in mediation..."* The report alludes to discussions but lacks analysis or explanation. It would have been helpful to learn the substance of those discussions, what strategies were considered, why they would make an effective defense, and what, if any, conclusions were reached.

b. *"Our discussions were focused on limiting XYZ's exposure at time of trial..."* Knowing what the discussions actually considered would have been useful. After all, limiting a defendant's exposure at the time of trial is certainly something the defendant/client would heartily endorse as it is the basic, perhaps, only goal of each and every defendant. Which raises several questions: *What were the options under consideration? Which options were deemed to be most helpful in limiting exposure? What path to achieving that limitation was selected as the one most likely to achieve a good result? Why was the chosen option considered the most likely to succeed?* Why does the report make such a mystery of the important details?

c. *"Plaintiffs view it as a great benefit to have XYZ at trial also arguing..."* Why? Surely they have understood the arguments, and are capable of making them without help. Is there a reason they believe XYZ, a defendant, should remain involved and dealing with the continuing risk of a runaway verdict as well as incurring significant trial expense? What is that "great benefit" other than the obvious ones of having XYZ bear the cost of experts, and perhaps get hit for a much bigger verdict than anticipated. Note that it is Plaintiffs' counsel who think it is a "great benefit," obviously, for Plaintiffs. What does XYZ's counsel actually think of Plaintiffs' view that XYZ should participate at trial? Does he also agree it is "a great benefit" to have to appear at trial and mount a full defense? Again, no analysis, no discussion, no clue.

d. *"We would anticipate such experts would be focused on issues of the toxic fume release and navigation..."* Setting aside the vague and repetitive language, one yearns to hear exactly what are those "issues" on which the experts will focus. Indeed, if the experts are to give testimony, one wonders what conclusions they have reached, and what problems they anticipate in presenting evidence and making the case for the defense. Even if the experts' reports were not yet available, counsel should surely know what questions he will ask, and what answers he anticipates the experts can provide in aiding the defense.

e. "*We summarize the results of our recent efforts below.*" But there is no summary, just a few vague statements. And even if the report had included a true summary, why waste a sentence saying so. In a lengthy report, use a subhead; something clever like "SUMMARY." As a general rule, if the report is three pages or more, a summary paragraph or two is often helpful to a client, especially someone who may have to read hundreds of reports a week. That summary should start with a one-sentence background, e.g.,*"The master of the M/V OIL SPILL, after imbibing a fifth of adult beverage, passed out on the bridge and ran the ship aground on the Pedro Bank off Jamaica."* This should be followed by a statement of the important conclusions that follow. It's obvious in the report above that the verbosity is a ruse to inflate what should be a note of, say, 10 lines, into a two-page exercise in double-speak. If you have something to say, say it. No need to *say* you have something to say.

Which brings me to **Grayson's Rule**:

When reporting to client, never, ever, refer to discussions, analyses, strategies, conclusions, agreements, propositions, ideas, understandings, or considerations without stating exactly what they are and how they impact the case. If those events don't impact the case, why bother mentioning them? Unless you're trying to convince your client she is paying for some real action even if that action is not revealed. And why would you want to do that?

Reporting depositions is a special circumstance that is governed by many of the same rules of simplicity and clarity, although there are many acceptable and effective styles.

As a rule, it is a good practice to start your deposition report with a general impression of the witness. A jury will be looking at, and listening to this person, and will consider his or her appearance and presentation in weighing the value of their testimony. There is no need to draft lengthy paragraphs that detail the witness' apparel, education, vocabulary, or posture, especially if it is appropriate to and expected of such a person.

Start with a general impression of the witness.

I once deposed a shrimper, a crewman working for a share of the profits on a Louisiana shrimp boat. A sturdily built man with trimmed gray hair, he was polite, articulate, and focused. A jury was going to believe this person. I believed him. What's more, I had the feeling if you put him in a double-breasted pinstripe, you could send him to the US Senate and half of America would believe him. That was worth mentioning in my report. On the other hand, the same demeanor, appearance, and presentation in an expert economist would not be mentioned at all. Now, if the economist showed up for deposition in torn jeans and seemed barely literate, that would be worth mentioning.

There is also no need to repeat, "*she said*" for every comment. The heading of your discussion paragraph will be: **Deposition of Captain Jolly Roger**. Your client will understand you are reporting what Jolly had to say.

There is also no need to report at length if the testimony merely repeats or reinforces what has already been related to the client. That is, a brief comment such as, "*Captain Roger testified in accordance with earlier reports and her testimony added little to what is already on record,*" might be the entire discussion. Of course, if the Captain raised even one or two points of interest, those should be noted. Further, you must describe and explain the import of every piece of evidence or testimony that has a meaningful impact on your case. For example, it may have already been related by another witness that the explosion originated at the production platform's bleed valve. If the Captain is the first to corroborate this opinion, that point should be mentioned. If several witnesses have already made the point, however, the Captain will have merely "testified in accordance with earlier reports."

You should conclude with one or two sentences which put the

testimony in perspective, and state whether your case was helped, hurt, or unaffected by what the witness had to say, and what further testimony is anticipated or may be needed.

Describe the importance of every piece of evidence (testimony) with a meaningful impact on your case.

Also, report dates first—especially the trial date—as soon as it is assigned by the Court ("*Trial has been scheduled for February 14, 2012, before a jury in Ketchikan, Alaska*"). And repeat the trial date as the first line of every subsequent report to client ("*Trial remains scheduled for February 14, 2012*"). This is important because all actions taken in defense or prosecution of a lawsuit, all strategies devised, and all efforts undertaken, depend on and are driven by the trial date. Settlement opportunities, Motion practice, discovery, all are hostage to the trial date. So that date should be your guiding light. Your strategies and settlement posture will vary depending on the imminence of trial.

Report to Client/an Outline

The following is the framework of an actual report to client, using standards I find most useful in my practice. You'll find in the Appendix a complete, 12-page report, which may be used as a template for comprehensive reporting:

Ms. Sophia J
World Claims Adjusters
11707 Wilshire Boulevard
Los Angeles, CA

Re: X Industries v. ABC Ins. Co. & Broker
Your Ref: 123 A 398
Our Ref: 2157 06 2373

Dear Ms. J:

The Court has continued Trial of this matter until 21 June 2012.
The final Pre-Trial...

<u>FACTS</u>

Our client Broker provided Property coverage to X Industries through ABC Insurance Company. The policy... with exclusions for product loss or damage due to defective workmanship... X Industries has brought suit against ABC Ins. Co. and Broker, claiming the policy should cover...

<u>SUMMARY</u>

I expect defendant ABC Ins. Co. to be dismissed at hearing on its Motion for Summary Judgment on calendar for December 12, 2012. Moreover, I do not believe Broker has significant exposure...

Damages are claimed to be over $700,000.00 for unusable product and $6 million in loss of business and diminution in value of X Industries as a result of...

With your authority, we have made a nuisance value offer in an attempt to open a settlement negotiation. We await a counter demand from Plaintiffs.

<u>LITIGATION STATUS</u>

A stay on discovery had been in effect until lifted by the Court on 19 August 2011. The stay was instituted while the Court was considering ABC Ins. Co.'s Motion for Judgment on the Pleadings which, if successful, would have resulted in an immediate determination...

At hearing, the Court ruled on a technicality that grounds did not exist... position was, technically, correct, the Motion was denied.

Now that discovery is open, we have noticed the deposition of Plaintiff X Industries' Person Most Qualified to testify as to various aspects of the claim.

A copy of our Notice is enclosed...

Because X Industries was sold by the P's subsequent to bringing suit, I would not be surprised for X to claim they are no longer in possession of documents relating to the loss. At that point...

LIABILITY

...there is not a large body of law which directly addresses the issues raised here. Most decisions dealing with defective products arise from traditional, third party, product liability claims, not property claims for "defective manufacture." Over time, and several appearances testing legal issues...

In the case of Parallax Productions v. Pancoast Underwriting, 16 Cal. App 4th 333 (2004)...

We have also found cases [e.g., Sympatico Products v. Dynastic ABC Ins. Co., 437 F. Supp. 233, C.D. CA (2005)] which allow an insured to recover for damage to an insured's own property caused...

While we believe that, ultimately, the Court will determine there is no coverage for the loss, it is the professional negligence and breach of implied contract claims against our insured that are more troublesome...

DAMAGES

The damages claimed are substantial. X Industries alleges it had to destroy and discard over $600,000.00 worth of stock consisting of valves and hoses. Moreover, it claims...Based on the scant documentation provided...the gross revenues of X Industries totaled $1.6 million...

As for its claim for loss of business and diminution of corporate value, it is clear X Industries depended on rather creative accounting practices to avoid showing an annual profit. Thus...

SETTLEMENT

As per our agreed plan, because Plaintiffs' counsel was unwilling to make a demand, we...

STRATEGY

I expect plaintiffs' testimony at deposition will proclaim X Industries was assured by Broker that if X Industries made a defective product, as in this case, coverage would be provided...I expect we shall prevail on the coverage issue... Legal research we have conducted...

As for the issue of professional negligence...

EXPERTS

I think it is becoming increasingly likely this case will proceed to trial. If settlement is...

DEPOSITION OF JOHN DOE, CPA

Doe, the accountant for X Industries, testified in accordance with reports previously analyzed...The one significant point of departure from the reports in Doe's testimony concerned the...

BUDGET

I propose the following budget for your consideration. Of course, these parameters are only estimates but I would expect the final figure to be close to this total. I trust you will...

LEGAL		
Fact Investigation/Development/Reporting	hrs.	$
TRIAL		
Preparation	hrs.	$
Fact Witnesses	hrs.	$
EXPENSES		
Experts fees	hrs.	$
Mediators/Arbitrators	hrs.	$
Deposition transcripts	hrs.	$
TOTAL		$

We shall, of course, continue to monitor this action closely and report significant events to you.

Very truly yours,
Martin L. Grayson

CHAPTER 12

E-Mail is Not Your Friend

Some client matters are obviously privileged, but you still don't want to put those matters in writing because the recipient—or someone in their office—may not realize the matter is privileged. Before you know it, the document has been faxed in error to the wrong people.

Think it doesn't happen? Wrong.

It happens all the time.

I cannot be certain that my own office has never mistakenly sent a privileged document (a report to client, or letter to an expert) to a party who shouldn't have received it. But I do know I have received faxes and e-mails sent to me in error. And I know for a fact that many of my clients have sent messages—even if just as intra-office e-mail—which amounted to admissions of gross irresponsibility if not admissions of legal liability. Of course, at the time the toxic e-mail was composed there was no loss, no claim, no law suit. It was just another day at the office!

In fact, this morning I read an e-mail from an insurance broker to his in-house account manager/assistant. It said in part, "*I am a negligent, careless, and self-important person, please sue me.*" Well, at least that was my interpretation. The actual wording went something like this:

> *"Sorry, I have been very busy this week and didn't have chance to look at the X Industries insurance renewals. I've been working on two major accounts and will get around to X when I have some time."*

Why would anyone make this admission in writing? At any time? To anyone?

If you have to put something in writing, how much smarter to write, "*X Industries is top of my list. Getting right on it.*" Of course, that would have required careful thought, which is precisely why e-mail is often so objectionable; its very informality puts the emphasis on speed over consideration.

Toxic e-mail. Just another day at the office.

Before leaving this example, I should point out that the broker's mindless e-mail was in response to an equally mindless prompt from the assistant. It went something like this: *"Joe, we may have to cancel your three-martini lunches this week, at least until you finally get around to taking a look at X Industries. Renewal is a just a few days away."*

When it comes to e-mail, think Enron; think US Justice Department.

E-mail is *not* private, *not* privileged, *not* your friend.

Advise clients to assume everything they put in writing will be seen by someone who loathes them, and who is looking for ways to put them out of business and to make their lives miserable, in addition to making them pay mega-dollars for the honor of being named e-mail Dunce of the Year. Because that is what most litigated cases and many business relationships sometimes become; a test of wills in which every available weapon and every scrap of ammunition can and will be used in battle. Why go out of your way to arm and equip your adversary?

Thus **Grayson's Corollary Rule:**

> Never, ever, put anything personal or unrelated to business in business/office communication of any kind.

If you want to e-mail your Mom some personal thoughts, we encourage the practice...unless, of course, Mom is a client and you also intend to refer to business.

No matter how much of a friend a client might be, no matter how much fun you had duck hunting or bowling or playing golf with that person last week, business correspondence is for business. And an innocent, friendly comment in an otherwise completely professional message can make you look like a reckless pirate in the hands of an experienced litigator; that is, the one who has decided to sue your client for some reason, no matter how absurd.

Here's how it might go down:

Q: *So, Ted, in response to Mr. Jones' urgent inquiry, you sent this e-mail, Exhibit 5?*

A: *Yes, sir.*

Q: *You responded immediately because of the importance and urgency of the matter?*

A: *Correct.*

Q: *And this matter had your full and complete attention?*

A: *Yes, sir. It sure did.*

Q: *Well, Ted, do you consider a golf game as important as the proxy issues facing Mr. Jones and his company?*

A: *Of course not.*

Q: *Why then, might I ask, did your e-mail include this line, "Great to see you on Sunday, Mel, even if you did beat me with that par on 18."*

A: *I was just trying to be cordial.*

Q: *So you were focused on cordiality rather than the proxy issues?*

A: *No, sir.*

Q: *But since you took the time to mention the golf game—at the very beginning of your message, I might add—you would understand if the jury reached the obvious conclusion you were not giving your full attention to the problems facing my client's company and were just as interested in your golf game?*

Many clients send email that amounts to admissions of gross irresponsibility if not legal liability.

How would *you* answer? More important, why would you put yourself in this position in the first place?

Why not just send a second e-mail complimenting Jones on a good round; an e-mail that doesn't mention business at all? That way, the golf e-mail isn't part of the file, and won't be paraded before the jury at trial. After all, your great lunch with George is entirely and completely separate from your work life and should not reflect on it in any way. It's impossible, of course, to keep people from saying stupid things, but at least they can be prevented from doing so in writing.

I suggest that you and your clients avoid problems by confining e-mail to its simplest function—delivering information; e.g., *"The status conference is Wednesday, May 2, 2012, Department 62, Central District, 8:30 a.m."* Or, *"John Doe arrives at LAX on United flight 110 at 7:15 p.m. on Tuesday, March 16, 2012."* Or, *"Thank you for your transmittal of documents in the referenced file."* Anything else—requests, questions, explanations, advice, analysis, conjecture—should be dispatched in correspondence or reports that have been drafted, edited, revised and, most important—and most often overlooked in e-mail—seriously contemplated, considered, given some THOUGHT.

The illusion of productivity

Not only is e-mail neither private nor privileged, it isn't the efficient time-saver everyone thinks it is.

If you are honest, you will have to admit that for every clear, well-reasoned e-mail you receive, you get dozens that are utter nonsense.

Think of all the times—perhaps many times a day—you read an e-mail that requires you to hit the "Reply" button, asking for explanation, clarification, or more information. Sometimes these tennis matches go on for weeks. Each time the ball lands, someone has to read the new message—often along with nine or 10 automatically repeated messages! Then, after concluding that nothing can be done, the ball is sent back across the Internet to the sender (and the 12 cc'd parties) with another non-response. It might feel productive, but it's just a lot of busy work.

Perhaps that's why e-mail is so popular. It lets you *feel* productive when all you're doing is defining why you can't be productive.

I sometimes am required to review page after page of e-mail correspondence in which nothing of substance is said, no issue is coherently or directly addressed, no thought is clearly expressed, no theory contemplated, no plan suggested. Just page after page of bouncing the ball back and forth so everyone feels they are hot on the case, up-to-date, productive, and responsive.

In my opinion, e-mail should be shunned by serious business people or used only rarely for safe, informational purposes.

Or, if you don't have time to give a matter real thought, undertake real analysis, and compose a clear, unambiguous presentation, then say nothing. At least you will have said nothing in writing! If the matter isn't worthy of in-depth analysis, a simple phone message or spoken reminder will suffice. If, as the account manager, you think you have to put something in writing to cover your own position, make it something businesslike and functional, such as, "*Hi Joe. Please advise on status of X Industries renewal*" (omitting any reference to three-martini lunches).

My advice: Avoid e-mail whenever you can, and note the increase in your productivity and the decrease in your level of frustration.

The wayward e-mail

I have sent e-mails that *appear* to have been delivered without error, but which my clients swear they never received.

In fact, on the day I was revising this chapter an opposing attorney faxed me—at my request—seven pages comprising five e-mails he claimed to have sent me over the preceding two weeks. I never received a single one. Upon review, it appeared to me the address he used was correct on only one message and incorrect on two. The last two messages appeared to be intra-office memoranda, and I couldn't figure out what e-mail address was used.

The same day, a client called to ask why I hadn't responded to e-mail he sent a week earlier. When he faxed the entire message to me, I noticed that the e-mail had been sent to "*awgrayson,*" probably ending up in the hands of someone named A.W. Grayson, instead of to one of my addresses. Whoever sent me the e-mail—probably my principal himself—had evidently not depressed the "L" key hard enough. So, the message went to *awgrayson*, and there followed a week of hard feelings and irritation for my client, in the midst of my own blissful ignorance.

Electronic junk mail

I am unaware of any direct research, but I am reasonably certain that a letter received by "snail mail" is read quicker and more carefully than a letter received by fax, and both are read in a more thoughtful, timely manner than anything received by e-mail. To a large extent, even serious business e-mail has become electronic junk mail. And, as I don't consider my work to be junk—especially not my reports to client—I refrain from using e-mail for that purpose. E-mail is a neat toy, and like most toys is best used for play.

But good writing and clear thought take time. Here's an example of an e-mail that contained neither good writing nor clear thought, and that I received from opposing counsel the other day:

"*Hi Martin. Please let me know where things stand on your end as we want to keep moving forward. Best, Henry.*"

What does he mean? Where do I stand on what? Move forward? Did he think I wanted to move backward?

Or...does he really want to know about the status of discovery, the prospects for settlement, news about my intended office relocation, or the state of the economy? If so, why didn't he ask?

Naturally, I filed Henry's e-mail in the correspondence folder (firm rule), and then ignored it. If Henry couldn't spare the time to compose a clear, concise statement of his concerns, it was presumptive of him to expect me to take the time to try to read his mind and agonize over what he really meant to ask or wanted to say. Henry knew where to find me if he had something worthwhile to discuss.

I must admit that, on occasion, I, too, have started composing an e-mail, thinking I could quickly spin off a sentence or two and present myself as Mr. Efficiency. It usually happens if a client e-mails me their request for an update on the status of their case. By the time I spin off that sentence or two, though, I realize I must stop, draft a coherent, comprehensive response, and put it in letter form and fax or mail it, e-mailing it as an attachment only if the client insists.

But that's me.

If speed is all you care about, then perhaps an unedited, unconsidered, seat-of-the-pants e-mail is the way to go. But you might first consider what Voltaire, that famous French essayist, wrote on this subject three centuries ago: "*Forgive the length of this letter,*" he said. "*I would have made it shorter but I didn't have the time.*"

Memorandum

From: Martin L. Grayson
To: Staff
RE: E-mail procedures

1. Do not use e-mail if any alternative means of communication is available.
2. Even if the Re: refers to the case name, the text header should contain the file number, addressee's file number, if known, and the date.
3. All e-mail must be marked "From" and "To" fully identifying the addressee, and all copied persons, and their affiliation.
4. Only one file matter or account may be discussed/referenced in any single e-mail.
5. If e-mail must be used, it is best to restrict the text to purely informational/fact matters, e.g., "This will confirm we are to meet on Monday, 9/21/12 at 2:00 PM."
6. Personal notes should never be included in a business transmission. It trivializes the business and makes it seem like social matters are of equal importance. If you must send a personal message, send a separate e-mail.
7. E-mail, like all other communication, must be in complete, clear sentences. "Etc." doesn't mean anything or, worse, it means whatever another party (or their attorney) may wish to imply it means.
8. References to telephone conferences or face to face conversations should include the date, the parties involved and a clear statement of what was discussed and agreed. (Example: "Thank you for your telephone advice of 3/16/12 that the insured has received written notice of the mediation scheduled for 10 May 2012," rather than, "Thanks your advice re mediation."
9. There is a tendency with e-mail to assume the reader is viewing the exact same documents and understands the exact same facts that you do. This is inappropriate and often mistaken. Every written statement you make, especially in e-mail, should be complete and stand alone. (Example: "We agreed in our telephone conversation of 2/16/12 that our initial offer at mediation would be $75,000," rather than, "Confirming our talk re: Mediation, let's proceed," or, as often seen, "Okay, let's proceed."
10. See 1.

CHAPTER 13

Handling Opposing Counsel

Dealing with opposing counsel is an art usually requiring years to perfect. And yet, it can actually be summarized in a single concept: *Do unto others as you would have them do unto you... until proven otherwise.*

First, assume that opposing counsel will be—like you—a decent, honest, diligent, professional problem-solving machine who understands that his job is to help clients solve their problems ethically and honestly with dignity, integrity and courtesy. Of course, it's entirely possible this assumption will be incorrect.

Opposing counsel could be a lying, cheating, perjury-suborning, drug-abusing, Unabomber-wannabe. But assuming the worst at the outset—especially when based only on the fact that he is your opposition—is guaranteed to make the litigation a nerve-wracking, back-stabbing war of undignified scrambling and shoving for crumbs of procedural advantage. Of course, some cases may devolve to this miserable state despite your best efforts. But your initial contact with opposing counsel should always be cordial and respectful, no matter how misguided their lawsuit or defense or negotiating position in a transaction.

For starters, I always act toward opposing counsel as if we were pals, buddies. If you have a specialized practice—e.g., intellectual property, mergers & acquisitions, trusts and estates, oil & gas—you likely will be running into the same firms and the same attorneys again and again, even in the largest markets. There will be some counsel you like more than others; some you will find easier to work with than others. But the very fact of familiarity—your knowledge that opposing counsel has been here before and will be here again—makes the initial contact more relaxed.

Try to take the same posture, even with counsel you are encountering for the first time.

If they are experienced and professional, they will immediately recognize the same qualities in you, and you will have taken a great first step toward making a new friend and—more importantly—obtaining a good result for your client. Even if they are the type of slimy creature that sometimes makes us ashamed to admit we are attorneys, your cordiality will pay dividends. In fact, I have found the sleazier the ambulance chaser, the more they appreciate being treated with respect; as a result, the easier it is to help my client. So what if opposing counsel is rude and arrogant. Behave collegially, and they will bask in the glow of being treated like an esteemed colleague. They will feel good. They will like you. And that is good for your client!

Do unto others as you would have them do unto you... until proven otherwise.

Now, maybe, you really do consider yourself too good to shake the hand of an attorney who spends his time recruiting "accident" victims from among the members of his old motorcycle gang, and has been suspended from practice several times for various lapses in ethics and manners, as well as mistakes in accounting and observation of the drug laws. In that event, it might not be easy to treat old Harvey with cordiality and respect, but I advise you to do so. Not only will this attitude be good for your client in several ways—from end result to reducing the expense of the litigation—it will also make your life a lot simpler and less stressful.

BACK STORY #1

Speaking of Harvey...

I had Harvey the Harley Guy as opposing counsel in a case a few years ago. It involved an unwitnessed "accident" that was supposed to have occurred on an oil lease where someone—allegedly my client, the lease owner—left a padlocked gate open across a dirt-and-gravel access road at the time a motorcycle gang member just happened to be rolling down that road and, allegedly, struck the gate. Although there were no physical injuries (at least none that could be distinguished from those he sustained in a bar fight the night before), the biker was claiming permanent brain damage.

I probably don't have to tell you these folks were not straight shooters. They did not deserve much respect, but I gave them all I could. In fact, Harvey and I became such good pals that he used to prance around like a pet waiting for a treat. I'll never forget his cornering me after his client's deposition.

"He was okay, right? A nice guy. I bet you were surprised, right?"

My response was genuine.

"Well, Harve, you did make sure he took a shower recently, and he was wearing a nice, new long sleeved-shirt buttoned up to his nose so his tattoos were covered. I'm not sure that makes him a good guy, and I'm not sure I believe everything he had to say. Heck, I'm not sure he believed everything he had to say, but you did a fine job."

Harve was all smiles.

Later in the case, Harve was suspended 30 days by the Bar for various moral and economic lapses. But we had now become such good pals, he felt comfortable calling to tell me that I might get some correspondence or pleadings from his office "assistant." Not he himself, of course, because he was not actually practicing during the suspension, and please don't tell the Bar. *Sure, Harve. I understand, Harve. By the way, why don't we settle this thing before you go into hibernation, Harve, old buddy*?

Harvey was so used to being treated like an orphan that being kicked one more time wouldn't have had any effect on him at all. To the contrary, it would have supported his view of big firm lawyers as stuck-up, egocentric pigs who don't give a darn about the common man, a mantle Harvey was pleased to carry. On the other hand, Harvey was so tickled to be treated as an equal, he later said he was thinking of asking me to represent him in one of his contretemps with the Bar.

Being friendly with opposing counsel always yields benefits, especially in personal injury litigation. For example, on more than one occasion, representing defendants, I would manufacture excuses to travel with plaintiff's counsel. In the case of the injured Michigan deck-hand mentioned in Chapter 2 (Depositions), plaintiff's counsel and I were flying in from different cities for the Michigan depositions. But I arranged to rendezvous at the Detroit airport so we could drive together to Grand Rapids. En route, we didn't discuss the case at all, but I learned a lot about counsel's tennis game and his kids. And, I like to think, that with seven defense targets at which he could have taken aim, my own client assumed a somewhat lower profile as a result of that long drive.

Behave collegially with opposing counsel; it's good for your client.

In my dealings with opposing counsel, I'm often reminded of what I learned in the practice of judo. One lesson in particular: Keep your opponent off balance.

My *sensei* (teacher) often reminded us that any encounter with the opposition involves combat, and it was no stretch for me to see that—in our work as lawyers—such encounters could be in court or across the negotiating table. So, when your opponent pushes, you pull; when they pull, you push. Keep your opponent off balance. Never provide a solid, inflexible target. This instruction just as easily relates to the give-and-take of ordinary conversation, courthouse hallway talk, contract negotiation, and, most especially, settlement talks.

BACK STORY #2

I once represented a steel manufacturer who hired workers through a labor contractor.

One day, one of the contractor's laborers was struck by a bundle of steel beams being lowered into a rail car for shipment. Plaintiff survived the accident, but suffered a crushed chest. Normally, the case would have been worth a lot of money. But because the worker was a "borrowed servant," and working under the control of my client, we probably had a good defense for Workers Compensation benefits as the exclusive remedy.

I met opposing counsel for the first time at the deposition of the injured man's primary treating physician. At that time, Counsel proceeded to lecture me on the prominence of his firm, how they only took major cases, how they routinely obtained multi-million dollar bad-faith judgments against insurance companies, and how they never settled a case for less than six-figures. I sensed that I was up against someone who fancied himself as King Kong, ready, even anxious, to crush any lesser mortal in his path.

At times like these, a little self-deprecating humor goes a long way.

"*Six figures?*" I said, shaking my head. "*Must be some mistake. My client would never trust me with a case that was worth more than $10,000!*"

King Kong and I proceeded through the day without exchanging another word about the value of the case. As I recall, it ended up settling for $20,000; nuisance value less than the cost of defense.

Remember, keep your opponent off balance. He pushes, you pull; he pulls, you push.

Another example:

One of my first office landlords was Andy, a successful plaintiff's personal injury attorney who owned the building where I opened my first office as a solo.

Andy had real estate holdings all over Los Angeles. But when the market cooled in the early 90's, he found himself "upside-down" on many of his commercial holdings having continually refinanced to buy more buildings. For a year or so, Andy paid a big firm to wrangle with a *megafirm* specializing in mortgage banking law that represented lenders. Now, in an effort to save money, he asked me to take over the case…even though my knowledge of real estate law was close to nil.

Keep your opponent off balance. They push, you pull; they pull, you push.

I accepted.

So, here I am with a case I had picked up on the fly, and I'm dealing with a mega-firm and a Heavy Hitter Name-Partner with a reputation for cutthroat tactics. Did Andy hire me to save money, or because he knew there was no hope, so he might as well stall and hide assets, file for BK, or flee to Rio de Janeiro?

Heavy Hitter and I spoke on the phone a few times and, before the next court appearance, agreed to meet for lunch (ostensibly so he could "bring me up to speed"). I tried preparing for the meeting as if I had a valid position to defend. But in fact, I had no weapon—not even a slingshot—to defend my client against Goliath. My only hope was to grovel and beg. Maybe Heavy Hitter would consider Andy and me so insignificant he'd refrain from stepping on us because he didn't want to take the time to wipe the bottom of his shoe.

As I drove to the meeting, I worked on my Total Capitulation Script.

Suddenly, I remembered the words of my judo instructor: *Keep your opponent off balance.*

It was good advice, but what if you have only five minutes to prepare?

Just then, on my car radio, I heard the sultry voice of pop singer Sheena Easton, and it produced the strangest epiphany of my life. Maybe one day I'll get a chance to thank Ms. Easton personally, because I suddenly knew how to handle the meeting.

When I got to the restaurant, I saw Heavy Hitter. He was a big, tense man who was flanked by an associate/vassal/bodyguard/monolithic goon built like Mike Tyson. So, there I was, practically reaching over my head to shake hands with these two mortgage mafioso who are about to feed me to the fishes, when I made my play.

"Sorry guys, I may be a little distracted here. This is a BIG day for me. I'm leaving my wife for Sheena Easton."

Whoa. Everything…just…stopped.

Heavy Hitter and Goon stared at me, trying to decide whether I'm a wacko or whether they should introduce me to someone in their firm who does entertainment divorce law and we can all become friends and hang out together on weekends in Malibu.

A few seconds later, Heavy Hitter gathers his senses.

"*Oh,*" he says, "*Is this going to happen soon?*"

I shook my head.

"*Probably not,*" I said. "*Sheena and I haven't ACTUALLY met, but I just heard that sexy voice of hers on the radio, and marrying her is something I think I really need to take care of pretty quickly.*"

Heavy Hitter and Goon never recovered.

They had lost the high ground of righteous indignation and legal certainty. In less than a minute, my Sheena Easton gambit had reduced them from legal monoliths to celebrity-seeking commoners. And even after they learned I was gaming them, the mood had already shifted, and they understood I could not be squashed with attitude.

Keep your opponent off balance.

Don't be afraid to move the battle to a new arena if the one booked for the contest is one where you are guaranteed to be decapitated. Once an opponent is off balance, they are wary, they are hesitant, they are easier to move. And they can be dealt with.

CHAPTER 14

Strategies & Tactics

What separates master chess players from the recreational players who know how to play and occasionally win a game or two?

A *basic* chess player knows the moves and some strategy, and may even know the next best move. A *good* chess player sees what the opponent sees, and can visualize what might be his opponent's best move. But a *grand master* has the imagination, creativity, and psychological insight to get so far outside himself he not only can calculate what he would do in your position, but what you will do in your position. It might be the same thing the grand master would do in your place, but it might not.

In Court, as in chess, you have to contend with what your opponent is *likely* to do, not what you think he *should* do, and certainly not what you want him to do. To think like a competent lawyer, you need to be able to get outside yourself; to set aside your own and your client's wants and needs, and to look at things from a different perspective.

If you do not have the ability to see the world from another's point of view, it is imperative you work on developing that skill. It also helps if you can imagine the responses of others, AND be able to assign probabilities to what they might do given their perspective, their nature, their abilities, and their preconceptions.

In Court, as in chess, you must imagine what your opponent is *likely* to do.

In the next chapter, I'll discuss how your predictions of human responses can help you prepare for the responses of others, as well as shape and encourage those responses you want. Before we get there, here's a simple illustration of what I mean by getting outside yourself.

The scene is a routine settlement negotiation with exactly the same $50,000 offer:

Lawyer A: *"Tell your guy I got $50,000 to settle this thing, and to take it or leave it."*

Lawyer B: *"Bob, you're a good guy and, while I think your client may be overreaching here a bit, he's probably a good guy, too. I'm sure you'll be able to make him understand what I have to deal with on my side. I have a client who is huffing and puffing about never paying a cent and calling me a gutless sell-out for wanting to even talk about a settlement. They think, and I think, your case is not a winner, at any amount. I've tried to tell them there are costs involved, including my fees, even if they were to win at trial, as they fully expect. They just don't want to listen to anything having to do with a compromise. They are out to prove a point. I have, however, gotten them to agree to an offer and I'm pretty sure they might even go to $50,000 if that will end this thing. Anything beyond that, well ..." (accompanied by a sad shake of the head)."*

Whose approach is more likely to be effective (assuming you do want to settle the case)?

Lawyer A's approach is arrogant, self-focused, inner-directed, and almost guaranteed to result in rejection. I was once on a conference call when another attorney made almost exactly the same *take-it-or-leave-it* speech to plaintiff's counsel in a case we were jointly defending. On the other hand, Lawyer B has deftly moved the discussion away from just the money. Sincere or not, he gives the impression he's trying to reason with his clients, and that even though they think the other side's case is worthless, he wants to get opposing counsel's clients a couple of bucks and minimize their legal costs as well. Sounds fair. Certainly sounds more likely to actually start a settlement negotiation than a war.

One of the most difficult things for any human being—let alone accomplished lawyers—is to cede merit to an opposing position. Indeed, some consider it a sign of weakness, and perhaps even counter to advice offered elsewhere in this book to the effect that you must believe in your case and use every device available to make that belief sincere. Such a belief, however, does not mean you can ignore the fact there is another attorney, right there on the other side of your case, who has convinced himself to believe in his cause just as strongly as you believe in yours.

Your job is to find out why your opponent has deluded herself in that manner so you can prepare your counter attack.

At the very least, you must prepare a good defense or your cause is lost.

Jim McElhaney, a trial advocacy genius, wrote an article for the ABA Journal (2001) that provides an important lesson. The article focused on the issue of character—specifically the client's character—and he used the example of a large corporation that terminated an older, long-time employee without accommodation, reasonable compensation, or recourse.

In the article, Professor McElhaney's alter ego, a litigation zen master named Angus, turns to a young apprentice:

Angus: *Anyone older than Mr. Neesman get phased out?*
Apprentice: *No, sir, he was the oldest in the department by 10 or 12 years.*
Angus: *Any of the bookkeepers offered different jobs so they could stay with the company?*
Apprentice: *Five of the six moved to different departments.*
Angus: *So the only one who wasn't offered a new job was Neesman. Did they tell him why?*

After further give-and-take, all of it negative for the company which had behaved very badly, Professor McElhaney concludes: "*Nick* (the apprentice), *I'd say your client has a character problem.*"

Yes, indeed. And that problem will be presented to the jury at length, repeatedly. So, how do you deal with this problem?

First, you acknowledge it. And you acknowledge the reality that the problem will strike a chord with the jury beyond the facts and figures and testimony and statistics you intend to present in defense of the company. You cannot escape the attack by simply ignoring its potential for destruction or placing your faith in a token response, no matter how much you pray for that faith to be rewarded. You must face the problem and explain why it is not the important issue it might appear to be at first.

BACK STORY

I once represented a secondary defendant at trial resulting from an explosion at an offshore oil production platform. Several young workers were killed. Old George, lead counsel for the target defendant, a major oil company, planned to counter the horror of the young workers getting blown into oblivion by calling as a witness one of the company's production supervisors, a young man who often worked on the same platform. This likeable, clean-cut fellow had six young children. George's intent was to show the company as a family-oriented enterprise that would not knowingly put its workers at risk. Fair enough. But George's reliance on one likeable fellow with children as his only counter to the cruel deaths of several other young men was a form of denying the problem. George hoped this subtle suggestion of the company's wholesomeness would be sufficient to offset opposing counsel's constant hammering on the fine, brave, innocent young men who died that day only because, as he suggested, the oil company wanted to make a little more profit.

Needless to say, George's tactic failed, resulting in what at the time was the largest verdict ever returned by a jury in a wrongful death case in that particular U.S. District Court.

What could George have done differently?

Perhaps not much.

But, at the very least, he could have addressed the problem head on, acknowledging the tragedy of the accident, and then present his argument that even large oil companies—indeed, any company, large or small trying to make a profit—do not find it either humane or profitable to allow their workers to be harmed. To the contrary, George might have said, it hurts the company in many ways to lose any member of its family to death or injury no less for an older worker than a younger man. Furthermore, there is no profit that makes such a loss acceptable to the company, to any human being and the jury should understand that.

Maybe it's not a winning argument. After all, there was no chance this jury was not going to return a verdict for the plaintiffs. But it might have reduced the damages to reasonable, i.e., economically reasonable, numbers instead of the fairy tale figures that ended up on appeal.

The point is, you must not avoid preparing for, and facing squarely, the very best shot your opponent is going to take. You cannot bury your head in the sand, grasp at a straw, and persuade yourself that a likeable witness is going to offset the consequences of a major tragedy. As I said earlier, "*...you need to be able to get outside yourself; to set aside your own and your client's, wants and needs, and look at things from a different perspective.*"

It's what distinguishes Grand Masters from basic chess players.

CHAPTER 15

Settlement Negotiations

Once you're engaged in the "settlement dance," never allow your opponent to pick the tunes or establish the rules of engagement.

Use your powers of analysis and evaluation to determine a high, low, and medium result for your side, and then set out to make sure you end up on the low side if you represent the defendant and the high side if you are the plaintiff. As you develop skill in analysis, you will develop confidence in your judgment. This confidence will, in turn, strengthen your arguments and your positions, which your opponent will not fail to perceive.

What does it mean to establish the rules of engagement?

Here's a personal example:

Once, I actually showed opposing counsel a paragraph from a report I wrote to my client predicting counsel's initial settlement demand (see Back Story, Chapter 8). I shared my prediction with counsel for two reasons—to demonstrate his predictability and to rattle his confidence a little bit. What counsel couldn't appreciate, though, is that I was handing him a golden opportunity. But because he didn't know how to benefit, he was forced to yield his advantage. That is, by showing surprise that I was able to do his calculations and predict his analysis even *before* he did, he all but conceded that I was better at the game and probably better at litigation, better in the trial setting, and better at persuading a jury my client had the better arguments.

At that point, the case was won for my client even though I knew I would never force the case to trial because even a plaintiff's counsel with no confidence and a tremor in his voice was going to get more than $100,000 from a jury for an oilfield worker whose foot had been crushed by a pumping unit "horsehead" when it fell while being removed for replacement.

So, why did my early analyses (and counsel's concurrence) represent a golden opportunity for him?

Because the Tao of Settlement teaches us that *while you can never change reality, you can always suggest an alternative interpretation.* And, if you do so promptly and smoothly, you can retake the high ground.

If you were opposing counsel, how could you have taken the offensive in this example?

The correct answer is that you adopt the concurrent analyses as evidence of the obvious rectitude of *your own calculation,* at the same time turning an opponent's strength against him. Upon reading my prediction to my client, opposing counsel should have said something like this...

> *"Martin, I knew you were a good attorney, and it turns out you're an honest person to boot. My client and I reached the same figure because that is the clear value of the claim. It wasn't voodoo; it was common sense. Now, maybe you're going to suggest I was a bit generous to my client and you might be right. But we're in the very same ballpark. Heck, we're practically on the same base. And whether the final figure is $650,000—as I believe we can prove—or even just $500,000, we basically agree where this case should end up. I don't know if I can sell $500,000 to my client, but if you make the offer I'll see what I can do. Or we go to trial and, as you yourself have pointed out, I'll be asking that jury for at least $650,000."*

With this response, counsel would have accomplished two things:

First, and most important, he would have punctured my smug, self-satisfied balloon of superiority, and he would have quickly demonstrated he was not only unaffected—much less intimidated—by my prediction, he applauded its accuracy. Second, he would have brought the discussion to the very high end of his settlement dreams of greed and avarice. In fact, he and his client would have been dancing around the moon with even a $200,000 settlement (there were some contributory negligence issues that made this case less than a 100 percent sure thing), and here he was talking confidently about doing me a favor by accepting $500,000!

If you remember nothing else from this chapter, remember this:

Settlement is all about psychology and rhythm. The numbers are just the music in the background.

The Tao of Settlement starts with a dance that will end up where you want if you have that goal in mind before you take the first step.

So, start with your goal and work back to the beginning. Once you have analyzed the facts and the law, evaluated the case, decided where you could possibly end up (the high end for defendants, the low end for plaintiffs), where you most likely will end up (the middle ground)—and where you would love to end up (the high end for plaintiffs, the low end for defendants)—report to your client where you're headed…and start to dance. Your first move will be dictated by what you hope and intend to be your last.

Settlement is about psychology and rhythm; the numbers are just the music in the background.

The first evaluation you must make will be of judgment value. As discussed above, you need to assess the value of the case and do so dispassionately with due consideration of as many factors as you can identify. This figure is your best estimate of what a jury will tell you the case is worth, not what you and your client think is fair or what you and your client would like the jury to say.

For the sake of example, let's say you represent defendant and, having brought your powers of analysis to bear with singular intensity, conclude the probable jury verdict will be in the $400,000 range.

Your opening offer will be dictated by plaintiff's opening demand. If that demand is reasonable, you will want to encourage the dialogue (i.e., keep the dance going) by making a reasonable counter. Let's say plaintiff's counsel demands $500,000. You will immediately realize, in view of your own estimate of judgment value and conceding you may be a bit conservative by nature, that plaintiff's demand is not far from judgment value and signals counsel knows he will have to compromise that figure to avoid trial.

Based on your calculation of judgment value at around $400,000, you estimate the high/middle/low settlement ranges to be $300,000/$200,000/$100,000. If possible, you want to end up at $100,000 or less, but both you and, more important, your client, having digested and understood your clear and thorough reporting, believe

$200,000 would be an excellent result. What's your opening offer? It depends on several factors, but one thing is certain...it won't be $100,000. That's where you want to end up, not where you start. And it won't be $5,000 for that figure is unrealistic, an insult to opposing counsel who, very obviously, has persuaded her client to be reasonable as demonstrated by the opening demand of $500,000.

Note that a reasonable initial demand from plaintiff can be due to a number of factors:

- The most likely factor is that counsel has analyzed the case well and is being professional and reasonable about settlement.
- A second factor might be counsel's knowledge of facts or evidence not yet in your possession, and perhaps never to come into your possession, that diminish value in his calculation.
- Another factor could be counsel's fear of actually having to take a case to trial.
- A final factor might be inexperience (although I have found inexperienced plaintiff's counsel tend to grossly overestimate the value of their cases rather than underestimate). Similarly, inexperienced defense counsel tend to grossly undervalue cases, at least until trial looms a month away on the horizon.

Your opening offer will be dictated by your opposition's opening demand or offer.

Interestingly, after this section was first drafted, the ABA Journal ran an article focusing on the effect of tort reform in Texas on both plaintiff and defense firms. The article contained a sidebar describing the key points of the Texas legislation which restricted jury awards in certain personal injury cases and placed other controls on the litigation. One requirement, termed an "early offer of settlement" provision, requires the payment of some post-offer legal fees and costs by the party who rejects a settlement offer and then does not ultimately obtain a judgment near to or better than that offer or demand. For the defense, the Texas threshold is 120 percent; for plaintiffs, 80 percent. That is, if defendant offers $100,000, which plaintiff rejects, plaintiff must obtain an award of at least 80,000 to avoid paying the opposition's legal fees and costs from the date of the offer. On the other side, if plaintiff demands $100,000 which the defense rejects, then, at trial, the defense must lose no more than $120,000 in order to avoid having to pay plaintiff's fees and costs.

In effect, the legislature has passed a law which a knowledgeable attorney will quickly realize is aimed at making attorneys analyze and evaluate their cases with extreme care. [Note: California has a "Statutory Offer" provision which is very similar but does not include legal fees. As the prevailing party in litigation is routinely awarded some costs and expenses, however the "Statutory Offer" benefit is minimal and, thus, has little effect on settlement. It is most effective, in my opinion, simply in forcing counsel to relay the offer to his client when I suspect he might not otherwise be so inclined even though it is an ethical requirement.]

While the intent is clear and to be applauded, I believe the Texas standard is too strict. If there existed an Oracle of Objectivity that declared a case worth $400,000—and both plaintiff and defense counsel agree—that is still no guarantee a jury will agree. The Texas standard would start awarding fees and costs if a jury awards less than $320,000 (high reasonable settlement range) or more than $480,000 (high judgment value). Both jury awards, however, are within a reasonable range of evaluation. I would think one side or the other should be punished for being wholly unrealistic about the probable result, not simply a little too pessimistic or optimistic. That is, plaintiff's counsel may be dealing with a difficult client who, while he seems to understand her case is worth $400,000, is not willing to settle for that amount, but is willing to let a jury decide if he should get more or less.

Let's say the client wants $300,000 for herself; not an unreasonable desire. The offer is $400,000, of which the client will end up with about $250,000 after expenses and attorney's fees are deducted. Plaintiff decides to go to trial in the hope of getting a $500,000 judgment, a very possible result, especially in view of the 120 percent side of the Texas equation which allows a $480,000 award before fees and costs are granted. So, plaintiff proceeds to trial and the jury awards $300,000; again, not a bizarre result. But because the award is only 75 percent of the offer, penalties are imposed. That is a little harsh, in my opinion, because no matter how good an attorney might be at case evaluation I think it would be difficult to take that strong a position on these numbers and start to terrorize your client with possible sanctions.

On the other hand, in the same case, I would agree that sanctions are appropriate for a defense counsel who recommends no more than $200,000 in settlement for a case he believes is worth $400,000, or whose analysis is so shoddy he actually believes the case is worth no more than $250,000, and so proceeds to trial where he loses $400,000. Even though the sanctions are paid by the client, a plaintiff who convinces herself that her case is worth $500,000, and—simply because she wants that much—rejects an offer of $400,000, and then watches a jury award $250,000, might deserve some sanctions. But a jury award of $320,000 does not seem so out of touch with plaintiff's fantasy that punishment is in order.

Having noted that evaluation and analysis is as much art as science, I believe the margins for error should be a little wider than the Texas legislature has deemed appropriate. Put another way, attorneys should feel comfortable indicating to their client that the probable result at trial will not be 50 percent higher or lower than their evaluation. But taking a firm stand on a 20 percent margin of error? Maybe that happens in science, but rarely in art.

An unrealistically low offer should be made only when the demand is unrealistically high.

As to tactics, an unrealistically low offer should only be made when the demand is equally unrealistic on the high side.

Were plaintiff's counsel to have made a demand of $2 million, a $5,000 counter-offer should be tendered. While you await counsel's shriek of dismay and chagrin at your completely inappropriate and unrealistic offer, you can amuse yourself composing your response, which will be along the lines of,

> *"If you are referring to my client's counter-offer to your client's 'completely inappropriate and unrealistic' demand, I can understand your feelings. And, I would suggest that now we have gotten this silliness out of the way and the ball is in your court, please provide us a reasonable demand and we shall respond in kind."*

You can also make a low-ball offer simply to start the dance if you have been unable to get plaintiff's counsel to sit down and evaluate his case long enough to get an idea of value so that he can put forth a demand.

The lesson here:

If you respond to an over-the-moon demand with a reasonable

counter-offer—for example, $50,000—you are signaling your fear of the case, and your willingness to raise the stakes into territory where all the leverage is on your opponent's side. Note that few settlement negotiations end up at the 50 percent point, a straight split between the first demand and the first offer. If they did, all plaintiff's would demand $10 billion and all defendants would offer $1 and, even then, the case probably would not settle at $5 billion. Remember, too, as long as plaintiff or defendant is being totally unreasonable in his demands or offers, you have nothing to lose. If the case is worth $400,000, you will take it to trial every day of the week before you will pay $2 million in settlement. And, similarly, if you are plaintiff, you will go to trial every day and twice on Sundays before you will accept $50,000.

But let's say plaintiff's opening demand is $550,000.

This is a figure that deserves respect and a serious counter-offer. For one thing, we are now on firm settlement ground because anything close to a straight split between the demand and 0 is within your medium to high settlement range. At this point, it is likely the case will settle for less than $200,000. Your offer can range from $35,000 ($25,000 looks too contrived to be taken seriously) to $50,000, depending on a number of other variables, discussed below, and your relationship with opposing counsel.

On occasion, you will be negotiating with counsel you know from previous litigation and, having danced with this partner before, you will know some of her steps and she will know some of yours. Assuming there is a modicum of professional cordiality or, at least, some respect still remaining from the first go-round, the chances of settlement success increase if only because communication can be more direct and honest.

One thing I often do, as defendant, especially if I'm making what I consider a serious, respectful offer and not a nuisance value or low-ball figure, is to point out to opposing counsel my offer is a sign of respect for counsel and his case but is not an invitation to assume we can settle at the 50 percent midway point. With this comment, counsel is primed to understand settlement will not be likely for $250,000. The counter-offer here is an important one because it will likely signal whether this case, which will probably settle, will do so at the $200,000 level or less. If the counter-demand to a $40,000 offer, for example, is $400,000, then opposing counsel, whether he intends to or not, is signaling he expects to end up in the $200,000 to $250,000 range. If opposing counsel had made a counter-demand of $350,000, that would indicate counsel knows he will have to go below $200,000 to settle even if he would, no doubt, hope to keep the number at that level.

At this point, however, you have already brought the negotiation below the judgment value you have reported to your client and down to the point where your client will likely be saving money even if the settlement goes no lower. You should always point out to your client that early settlements also mean an end to legal fees and expenses with the resultant savings, a concept I have found very easy to sell to any client I have ever charged by the hour.

Tell your client that early settlements mean an end to legal fees and expenses.

If, after a $500,000 opening demand, plaintiff's first counter is $475,000 or $450,000, your response should be equally hesitant, perhaps only $10,000 to $15,000 more than your original offer. In this Pavlovian, stimulus-response manner, you are teaching opposing counsel that serious demands will be met with serious counter-offers but frivolous demands will be met with equally frivolous responses. While counsel still believes he is driving the negotiation, you, in fact, are establishing the negotiation parameters that will bring about the result you seek.

While all this is going on, however, you should communicate to opposing counsel in a manner calculated to reinforce his belief that he is in control and that you are simply a pawn in the hands of a difficult and impatient God, or client. For example:

> *"You know, Ted, when you made an excessive but still well-considered opening demand, I thought we might actually settle this thing. And I prepared my client to reach a little bit to accommodate you at a reasonable figure. Then you come back with an 'in-your-face, take-that-you-little-twerp'", counter-demand and my client thinks I'm a wimp and we shouldn't have gone on the table with $40,000 to begin with. Now you're making me look bad, and it was all I could do to get them to throw in another ten grand. I'm not saying there might not be some more there if we can get this thing done, but you've really put me in tough spot. I expect $50,000 isn't going to get this thing settled but unless we get some real movement my guys are going to say, the heck with it, take it to trial and see what happens.' If you're serious about settling this thing, you have to help me here."*

Remember, it's a dance. And, as with any performance, a little patter—and a great deal of psychology—should be part of the routine.

You could make an offer that says: *"Here's X, take it or leave it,"* if you want to guarantee the case will go to trial, a posture which, in my opinion, always works a grave injustice to your client who deserves an honest exploration of settlement possibilities. If you agree with the old saw that a bad settlement is better than a good trial, then a reasonable settlement should always be considered. Or, you can make the exact same offer of X in a way that signals you are willing to talk and trying to be reasonable. How will you know the other side doesn't want to dance unless you ask politely?

The psychology of litigation should never be underestimated.

While the facts and the law will generally dictate the results in almost all cases, the way the litigation is handled, the way opposing counsel is handled, and, most especially, the way the settlement negotiation is handled, depends as much on psychology as law. You ignore psychology at your peril, a theme first raised in my discussion of deposition technique (Chapter 2), and considered again when we looked at witness motive (Chapter 3). One very important aspect of the psychology of settlement harks back to our earlier discussion of judo techniques:

When *you* have leverage, push; when your *opponent* has leverage, pull. (Or, if you can't pull, run).

I make it my business never to talk settlement with opposing counsel after losing a motion, after a witness has testified effectively for the opposition, or after opposing counsel has returned from vacation and is feeling invigorated and ready to take on the world...and never, ever, after opposing counsel has won a big case. In fact, whether I'm plaintiff or defendant, I go on vacation myself, if necessary, to avoid taking her calls. But I do not speak to opposing counsel about settlement when she is still flush with the excitement and adrenaline rush of having slain the previous dragon.

The psychology of litigation should never be underestimated.

To the contrary, I like to wait until I have put some dents in an opposition witness; especially an expert.

I wait until my side has won a motion or obtained some interesting and helpful evidence, and I definitely spring into action when I have heard opposing counsel has gotten hit on another case. That's the time to be a friend and to go all out to "help" counsel settle your "little matter" before things get out of hand, or the clients turn adamant and trial is the only alternative.

Be confident, though, that no matter how bad your case, no matter how desperate your position, no matter how strong your opposition, there will be a point in the litigation when you will be at your strongest and opposing counsel will be at his weakest; when his slam-dunk case drops a rung from the top of the ladder. Whatever the reason—maybe just because he has a cold or his new Mercedes got dinged in the parking lot—there will come a day when counsel is not at his best, and that is the day you have to be there to be his good old pal. Everything may be against you, and maybe you are still going to pay too much or accept too little, but the best possible result you can ever hope to obtain will be on that day when there is a slight tilt in your favor.

So, be ready to act on that day and press your advantage to conclusion—no matter how small—as quickly as possible, and before King Kong wakes up and starts thumping his chest again over your fallen body. Don't be afraid to swallow hard and take the loss, especially if you can get any kind of a discount.

A corollary: You can always cave at the end. That is, if your ship is headed down with no survivors, there's no reason to speed the end.

In my opinion, cases settle on the courthouse steps only when counsel has not been able to recognize their high point.

I've settled cases on the courthouse steps, and it was always because there was nothing more I could do to tilt the board in my favor. Knowing you're going to lose and admitting to yourself you're actually going to lose are two different mind-sets. In the interest of providing your client with the best possible advice and saving as much of the client's money as possible, you have to believe in your own evaluation. If the case is a loser, you have to get out; the only exception being if it has to cost you a great deal more to get out than you conservatively estimate a jury will find. As in the illustration above, if plaintiff's counsel could elicit no higher offer than $50,000 on a case he was convinced had value in excess of $300,000, the case has to go to trial. Similarly, if the defense gets no demand lower than $600,000 for a case it has evaluated at no more than $300,000, you have to let the jury decide which side is right.

It is still the fact, however, that more than 95 percent of all cases settle before trial. So, while you should learn the art of war—and the subtle, psychological art of letting your opponent *know* that you know the art of war and do not mind employing it—you should also learn how to do the settlement dance.

CHAPTER 16
Mediation

Mediation is like tennis.

It's great fun and good exercise when you have a worthy opponent, but boring and tiresome when you play alone.

When preparing for mediation, your first consideration should be to determine whether your opponents will have brought their rackets or whether, feigning injury, insult, lack of coaching (authority to proceed) or other "unavoidable" circumstance, they are simply showing up to wave to the crowd (the mediator and the Court), and then head for the locker room.

Many cases settle at mediation.

Others consist of little more than one side or the other starting off by proclaiming the uselessness of the exercise. Then, only too anxious to prove themselves right, they take an irrational, nonsensical, unsupportable, all-or-nothing position, and stalk off when their good faith is questioned. You must be able to determine beforehand whether or not the opposition will be taking the mediation seriously, or you run the risk of exposing more than is prudent in a Mediation Brief (not to mention preparing thoroughly for a meaningful encounter that wastes your time and energy, and your client's money).

One way to ensure that the mediation is reported to principals, and will be taken seriously by the other side, is to require the physical presence of the party—corporate officer or insurance adjuster—with the authority to actually bind a settlement. At the very least, you can then be assured the persons to whom your opponent is reporting will have some knowledge of the status of the litigation, and will get to learn the details of your position, or as many as you choose to reveal.

Some states, such as California, require the physical attendance of parties with authority at Court-ordered mediation but, at voluntary mediation, a telephonic appearance is often permitted and, in practice, this often translates into an attorney doing what he or she thinks best and letting the principal know, by means of periodic telephone calls, how matters are progressing.

If personal attendance of principals at the mediation is not required or agreed, the chances of settlement drop dramatically.

If you cannot ensure personal appearances, you should—at the least—get opposing counsel to agree that he or she will have some authority to settle even before "consulting telephonically" with her clients during the mediation. That is, if the opposition is unable or unwilling to make even a nuisance value offer, or a less than 100 percent demand, why waste everyone's time and money with a charade? If opposing interests seem unwilling to agree to appear at mediation with some settlement authority, put it in writing that you believe the mediation should be postponed until such time as that will occur.

Mediation always begins with the mediator greeting the participants, and giving a general outline of the proceedings and his or her own preferred format. At this point, the telephonic attendees should be introduced. If not, you should make a specific request to do so. That way you can make certain there are, in fact, principals standing by with telephonic authority, and the mediation is not a sham. You want to ensure that opposing counsel sitting in the room with you is, in fact, talking to a real person with express real authority to settle the case, not just to a senior partner back at his firm who may be available, but who really has more important things on his mind.

Mediation is like tennis; good exercise when you have a worthy opponent, but boring if you're playing alone.

As for what to reveal in a Mediation Brief, be guided always by the belief that honesty is the best policy and the truth is the truth.

Of course, you need not reveal every piece of evidence you expect to introduce at trial, nor do you need to name every witness, and detail every fact on which you will rely. You should, however, establish a clear and reasonable position, and support it with enough evidence and cogent argument to persuade the mediator that you are the good guy. Remember, even a nefarious defendant may be the good guy if, through you, he demonstrates openness, displays a somber appreciation of all the facts, and then urges a path of cooperation, moderation, and reasonableness for all concerned. In other words, just because my client negligently sank the vessel and destroyed your precious cargo doesn't mean he should pay 10 times its fair market value. Sorry about that.

CHAPTER 17

Picking the Jury

When it comes to picking the jury, my advice is simple:

Pick a jury you like, pick a jury you think you can relate to, pick as members of the jury individuals you would want for friends assuming your universe was limited to the pool of jurors in the courtroom.

And when it comes to picking a jury, you should also have some background in the psychology of groups and the sociology of age cohorts.

For example, you should know that middle-aged Boomers are more liberal than either older or younger people. Which might seem counter-intuitive, except that Boomers were children of the Sixties, when social revolution and protest was rampant, marijuana was reasonably priced, and rock and roll (and French existentialism) was alive and well. And younger people, especially the 1980's-greed-is-good, Me-Generation types are usually more conservative than their parents.

Of course, these guidelines pertain to the hypothetical "average" person (if such creatures exist).

Each individual brings his or her own variables to the mix, and those have to be determined and weighed before a selection can be made. Statistical analysis based on such variables is the raw material for the conclusions of jury-metric consultants, the so-called expert advisers in jury selection. They have templates for age, residence location, occupation, marital status, etc., and they use this demographic information to predict a person's attitudes and opinions just as movie producers use demographic information to determine which movies teenagers will like well enough to see six times in the theater before buying the DVD. Just remember, though, that all the demographic information money can buy does not always translate into big box office. To the contrary, it does so only rarely.

Of course, if you are representing a six-time convicted violent offender on an armed robbery indictment, you do not keep a prison warden on the jury even if you think he's a pretty good guy. And if you represent a plaintiff in a personal injury claim, you do not want an insurance claims adjuster on the jury, even if she seems like a very reasonable and pleasant person. This is common sense and too obvious for further comment.

Beyond the obvious, however, my advice is "keep it simple."

Pick people you like.

And don't worry, you will find that you know who you like instinctively and almost immediately. With some jurors you'll like their look, their voice, their walk, their demeanor, the way they make eye contact, or the way they answer the judge's penetrating inquiry... "*Can you be fair?*" You may not know why you like them, and you probably would not be able to explain it to a consultant. But, if you like them, I say pick them, even if the demographics are not optimal.

In any event, jury selection has become so routinized and so perfunctory, with minimal questioning on *voir dire*—usually performed by the judge—that the process is practically worthless. In fact, many judges do not permit any questions by counsel other than to explore reasons for exclusion for cause.

According to most courts, if the prospective juror claims no relationship to the parties or their attorneys, no special knowledge of the facts, admits to no bias, and promises to be fair (and to try to remain awake until the proceedings are concluded), they are perfect jurors. Counsel might think differently, but they are rarely given the opportunity to ask questions which might allow them to make truly informed decisions about jury selection.

In the old days, a trial lawyer could chat with jurors about their likes and dislikes, the magazines they read, their educational background, whether any relative had recently sued an insurance company; all the things that would help you make an informed decision on their suitability to hear your case. But the "old days" are long gone. Now, only the most gentle, innocuous inquiries are allowed. The judge asks for an address, occupation, occupation of spouse, if any, and, if you're lucky, whether the prospective juror has been convicted of a capital felony in the last 30 days. And there you are.

So, this forced jury selection of more or less random beings has been countered by jury consultants who employ demographically-based statistical analysis to predict social attitudes and behaviors.

While I agree that demographics can be quantified to yield valid statistical conclusions, I believe it only works accurately for large samples. As for using computers to pick a jury based on age, occupation, income, etc., that is certainly a safe way to proceed. Then, if the verdict goes wrong, you made the best decision money could buy and no one would find fault with your method.

The finest trial lawyers rely on their instincts to recognize character types and preferences.

But many of the finest trial lawyers to ever enter The Well generally succeed by relying on their human, social experience, and a native instinct to recognize character types and preferences. They pick up on likes and dislikes through body language, eye contact, and a host of other factors which guides the human subconscious to prefer—even on a first meeting, and often within seconds—the company of one person to another. Computers can't do that.

If I had to select 50 out of 500 people to pitch a product or a lawsuit story line, determine a sentence for a convicted felon, or to vote for a certain candidate, I would be very comfortable depending on a computer and demographic analysis. I agree that a computer would probably select 50 individuals whose votes would be more likely than a randomly selected sample to go the way we preferred. Of course, not every one of the 50 would vote exactly as we desired, but even if only 35 voted our way as opposed to the 25 out of 50 that might be predicted from a perfectly random sample, that number (35–15) would be, statistically speaking as well as in the real world, significantly better than the 25–25 even split.

The trouble is, when picking a jury for the average civil or criminal trial, you will likely be picking, at most, 12 jurors from a group of, at most, 40 people. In such a small sample, the statistical probabilities don't have time to work. You could pick the 12 that the computer likes and no one would find fault. Or...you could pick the 12 you like, and the 12 who you think will like you.

The problem with using demographics to select a single human being—or 12—is that the minimum wage minority worker (a plaintiff's dream) may have a close relative who works for an insurance company (plaintiff's nightmare), while the CPA with an engineering degree (defense dream) may have a mother who was denied benefits by an insurance company (defense nightmare). Add to the mix the fact that some jurors actively try to fool the attorneys and the judge into choosing them or dismissing them, and the weight of the demographic analysis begins to diminish markedly.

It's like being unable to identify, much less control, all the variables in an pharmaceutical trial.

How can you reach a conclusion about the efficacy of a drug if you don't know whether all of your sample subjects in one group are two-pack-a-day, drug-abusing alcoholics, and all those in the other group are vegetarian aerobics instructors? The unknown variables are so powerful they obliterate what is of basic importance to the experiment; Group A got the placebo and Group B got the real drug. Again, even if you can't balance the groups, if the sample is large enough, the variables will even out. That is, the A Group and the B group will both end up with approximately the same number of junkies and fitness freaks.

But that's the point.

In court, you don't have a balanced, 400-person jury pool with equal numbers of Democrats and Republicans, college graduates and high school dropouts, drug abusers and teetotalers. And, even if you did, you wouldn't necessarily know. You may have 30 or 40 people, and a 12-person panel will generally come from the first two dozen, unless there are multiple defendants who each have several peremptory challenges to stretch the process. And you will likely never know which prospective juror hates corporations, or which one hates anyone who sues anyone else (unless they admit these biases, which a surprising number of jurors do in an attempt to be excused from the panel).

Cleverly, many judges get around this tactic by employing one of their own. They ask the juror if, in spite of their prejudicial history, the juror could swear to listen to the facts and then be fair in rendering a verdict. Now, it's one thing to admit to being biased. After all, as a potential juror, I might have good reason to be biased: Corporate America killed my pet hamster by having inadequate quality control at the pet food factory. Or, shouldn't I be allowed to hate plaintiffs because of the person who sued my company for age discrimination and sexual harassment, and now my company is in bankruptcy and I'm unemployed?

But ask that same person if they can be fair, and they puff up to full height and assure you there isn't a biased bone in their body. This is usually more than enough for a judge who knows that one or the other of the attorneys at bar will have to use a peremptory challenge to clear the room of all those "fair" people with an admitted agenda. The sooner the peremptorys get used up the sooner the jury can be empaneled, and the sooner the whole affair will be over.

Stick to the basics. Don't over-think what for hundreds of years has been a simple and instinctive process.

All of which is okay by the judge.

So I say, stick to basics. Don't over-think what has been, for hundreds of years, a simple and basically instinctive process. Decide who you like and—assuming there is no natural impediment to their selection which would allow you to have them excluded for cause, or an overwhelming factor which should outweigh their selection, even if they promise to be fair—go ahead and let them sit. And once you have decided to do so, do it quickly and confidently. It's a subtle way of letting them know you like them and trust them as opposed to the message you send if you hem and haw, whisper to your client, glare at them intently as if trying to read their soul, before finally saying they are acceptable to plaintiff or defendant.

The juror will appreciate the vote of confidence, and really doesn't have to know you are mightily ambivalent.

CHAPTER 18

Courthouse Demeanor

This is a story about human nature.

Imagine you're at a neighborhood party, having drinks with some friends. In walks Buddy, a neighbor who borrowed your ladder earlier in the day but forgot to return it. Buddy sees you across the room, waves, and shakes his head as if in apology for his lapse of memory. You nod and smile amiably, and turn back to your friends. who at that very moment are laughing at a shared joke.

Question: How likely is it that Buddy will assume the laughter is at his expense? Pretty likely. After all, you and the ladder in question are the focus of Buddy's most recent interaction with you.

In a roundabout way, this illustration goes to explain why you should never smile in the courtroom! Because those present in Court—the jurors on your case, the bailiffs, the clerks, the court reporters—will not know why you are smiling, *and may assume the worst.* They may assume—because it's only human nature—that it has something to do with the case that now occupies their attention, and they just might think your smile is about…them.

Don't underestimate the power of courthouse demeanor.

Don't smile in the courtroom, OR in the courthouse, OR even within a 10-block radius of your field of battle. Beyond that, you're on your own. You still might be seen by someone with a connection to your professional activities, but the odds are so small you should be free to run that risk and get on with your life. But within those 10 blocks, don't take the chance of giving someone a wrong impression that will neither enhance your image nor help you toward your goal.

Your demeanor inside, outside—and, yes, even around the courthouse—should be intended to persuade the judge, jury, bailiff, clerks, parties, witnesses, and anyone else who might be passing through, that you are a serious person, an honest person, a dignified person, an organized person and, for the purposes of the case at bar, the person with the correct view of reality. This image would be difficult to maintain if a juror walking through the parking lot saw you—where you thought you were out of sight—throwing off your suit and pulling on a pair of baggy shorts and a ripped T-shirt while chugging a 40 oz. adult beverage.

Don't underestimate the power of courthouse demeanor.

I can not emphasize strongly enough the importance of demeanor inside, outside, and around the courthouse.

Once there, assume there is a one-way glass and hidden microphone in every nook and cranny. A juror seeing you laughing in a hallway doesn't know you have just heard the best joke anyone ever told. They assume you're laughing about something in their case, something to which they are devoting their every waking hour, without laughing, because the judge has told them this is a serious business.

So, remember, anywhere in the courthouse where you might possibly be seen or heard litigating, negotiating, or consulting—through an office window, down the hall, in a restroom—should be an area where you are always on guard to present a professional image. Pretty much, that means anywhere in public.

The jury loves the judge

The judge is your friend.

Even if the judge hates you and you dislike him. You want the jury to form the impression that when you're not in trial, the two of you spend as much time together as possible, watching football, duck hunting, telling lawyer jokes. That's because the jury looks to the judge as the captain of their ship, the one force of truth and impartiality in a sea of subterfuge and duplicity. Even long after it becomes apparent (at least to you) that the judge has chosen sides and you are on the opposite shore, the jury will still think the judge is doing his job fairly and wisely.

So memorize this little ditty:

The jury loves the judge,
The jury loves the judge,
Hi ho alev-ee-o
The jury LOVES the juuuuudge!

Remember this for two reasons and cling to it:

First, the lyric is accurate. And second, if you forget that the lyric is accurate, you will be at sea without a life jacket. Even if the judge sprays your new suit with purple acid from a hose he keeps on the bench, you smile and bow and scrape and say, "*Thank you, your Honor.*" Your only chance of keeping the jury even partially on your side is to refrain from telling the judge what a political hack he is, and how you will regret to your dying day the $10 you contributed to his last campaign. You may feel better afterward, but always bear in mind that your client will be picking up the tab for your moment of joy.

You want to stay on the judge's good side.

In my opinion, one of the biggest mistakes an attorney can make is alienating the judge. You will put yourself and your client at risk of losing every close call, having every request for continuance or extension of discovery procedures summarily denied and, worst of all, having the judge signal the jury at trial that you are not trustworthy. Accordingly, my advice is, in the Courtroom, be as polite, obsequious, and humble as your nature will permit...certainly more than your nature might deem dignified. Fawning is not unacceptable, and bowing and scraping is not to be overlooked. I venture to guess there has never been a judge sitting on any bench, anywhere, at any time in history, who has admonished an attorney for being too respectful. Guide your actions, attitude, tone and language accordingly.

I was once at a CLE seminar on "The Elimination of Bias and Sexual Harassment" where the presenter described a scene that actually occurred between a judge and one of the attorneys involved with the case. When the presenter finished the hypothetical, he asked, *"So, what do you say to a judge who opens a Case Management Conference with the comment, 'That's an awful pretty dress you're wearing, little lady. And might I say you wear it very well.'"*

The answer was obvious. My hand shot up.

"*You say, 'Yes, your Honor. Thank you, your Honor. I was hoping you wouldn't think this dress was too informal, your Honor. Sir.'*"

You must realize that a Case Management Conference isn't about civil rights or the Constitution or truth, justice, and the American way. It's about serving your client. If the judge likes your dress, and you might be able to use that dress to persuade the judge that he should like your client, then—Neanderthal though I may be (and as politically incorrect as it may seem)—your response should be something along the lines of, *"You mean this old thing? Why, your Honor, I was afraid I'd look like a ragamuffin, but I had nothing else to wear. I'm so glad you don't think it's inappropriate."* As an early mentor once explained to me, "The judge may be right. The judge may be wrong. But the judge is always the judge."

Can't change it, so don't be offended by it.

In a criminal case, though, a little edginess to one's dealings with the Court might be tolerated because a jury expects the judge to be aligned with the establishment forces of the state. Moreover, it is part of the usual criminal defense tactic for attorneys to be counterculture in their look and behavior, thereby implying to the jury's subconscious that their client, also a counterculture figure (unless you live in a culture where drug abuse, armed robbery, and parole violation is the statistical norm), is really just a high-spirited kid.

Did you ever wonder why many male criminal defense attorneys sport pony tails, shaggy beards, and scruffy clothes, and female criminal defense attorneys wear shaggy hair, bright, attention-grabbing clothes, and a sarcastic, if not downright disdainful, sound-bite persona? It's their way of sending a subliminal message to society at large and the jury in particular that, *"Look, I'm kind of weird, I'm a little different, I may even be a bit of a jerk, but I'm part of the system. I'm an attorney for crying out loud. Just because you're a wacko jerk doesn't mean you're a criminal. So I think you should give bright, clean-cut, humble Jeffrey Dahmer here the benefit of the doubt. In fact, it's your sworn duty to do so!"* There are different kinds of dances for different kinds of courts, and if you intend to appear at the Criminal Cotillion or the Appellate Ball, for example, you should learn the steps.

Another point on courthouse demeanor:

Common sense tells you that court personnel are talking to the judge throughout the day, filling them in on what's going on in the courtroom when the judge is off the bench. So, it is safe to assume that your interactions with court personnel will find their way to the judge. Thus, in addition to keeping a polite, low-key, professionally calm demeanor in and around the courthouse, you must also ingratiate yourself with the courthouse staff. Believe me, it has its benefits. If, on occasion, you make a comment that elicits a laugh from another attorney, the clerk is more likely to take it in stride. And if the judge asks, *"What was that laughter in the courtroom?"* the clerk—your buddy—might be more inclined to say, *"Oh, that was Mr. Grayson. He's such a friendly and gracious person. I think he said something to cheer someone up and they were laughing a little,"* instead of that clerk saying, *"It was Grayson, Judge. What a jerk. He's here again today on GenMar. Number 6 on the docket. I don't know why you just don't find him in contempt and get him disbarred. Jail time would do him a lot of good."*

Assume your interactions (even gossip) with court personnel will find their way to the judge.

By the way, courthouse demeanor also extends to telephone calls!

I was in court the other day, and couldn't believe what I heard. An attorney on Court Call thought his phone was on "mute", and could be overheard babbling first to a buddy, then to an assistant, and then to various others, all while the judge was trying to conduct other business. Before the judge realized what was happening, and thinking counsel was talking to the Court, she twice advised him to remain "on hold" until his docket number was called. To no avail! Finally, the judge came right out and told him everything he said was being broadcast into the courtroom, and she ordered him to stand by, silently, until he was recognized. Counsel apologized, and then all of us in the courtroom heard him press the "mute" button, and launch into yet another round of office babble.

He had no idea his "mute" button had malfunctioned. The judge was not amused.

Grayson's Rule:

If you're on the phone to the Court during a Court Call, or for any other business, *assume you are actually in court and not simply in your office talking to the judge or clerk on a speaker-phone.*

If counsel had understood, he might have sat quietly at his desk, shuffling papers, reading the newspaper—even getting his shoes shined—but he would not have been making a fool of himself to the Court. As we have discussed at several points in this book, the psychology of human perception and the inferences drawn from them loom large in law and business. You have a lot to lose and absolutely nothing to gain from ignoring that fact.

Before we leave a general discussion of demeanor, some specific thoughts on dealing with judges:

In my experience, most judges hate to judge.

They do not want to make a call. They want you to settle your case, dismiss your suit, take the plea bargain, pay the demand. Judges do not want to have to actually decide anything if they can avoid it. But now, having read Chapter 3 (Witness Motive), you are uniquely positioned to use the judge's own motives to your benefit, i.e., getting the result you seek. How? By couching every argument in terms that fulfill and support the judge's most secret and fervent desire: To watch you dissolve into molecular space dust before the lunch break.

The techniques to employ in furthering your client's position should be obvious:

Every comment, every utterance, every suggestion must appear to be aimed NOT at winning or losing points for your team, but helping the Court resolve the dispute as quickly and painlessly as possible. Your comments should be sprinkled with introductions such as, "*In order to move this matter along as quickly as possible, perhaps ...*" Or, "*To give us the best chance to reach early resolution...*"

While your opponent flails around, arguing arcane points of law and procedure, he will find himself sinking in quicksand as you calmly and casually lead the judge to agreeing with your every suggestion. This is not to say you can be unprepared on the law and the facts and flim-flam the Court with obsequious comments. I'm simply suggesting you must carefully craft your arguments to avoid the common, "*Counsel is mistaken in his reading of Wizard v. Oz, your Honor, and is wasting the Court's time.*"

Rather, you remind the Court, "*Wizard v. Oz, which we sincerely believe counsel has been reading incorrectly, your Honor, does not get us past our problem of how to resolve the discovery issues here and move this case toward what all reasonable persons would agree should be an expeditious settlement or quick and amicable trial. With the Court's help, we should be able to cut through the delay and minutia of this legal skirmishing and get to substantive issues."*

The little ticking sound you hear will be the judge's heart going pitter-patter, pitter-patter.

CHAPTER 19

Ready, Your Honor

If you're an alert, conscientious lawyer, much of what you really need to know about trying a lawsuit will come to you the night before your first opening statement to your first jury. You will lie in bed for two or three hours, staring into the darkness with an awareness that is both frightening and awe-inspiring.

Lying there, you will see truth as never before with piercing clarity.

You will see every move you should have made, every question you should have asked, every exhibit you should have listed, every pleading you should have filed, every argument you should have prepared, every expert you should have retained, every witness you should have called; in short, you will see every single factor you should have analyzed, every action you should have taken, prepared for, and reported to your client. These images will appear to you floating in a globe of intense light like a brightly lit tableau in a dim museum. You will see the truth. And you will promise yourself that, if you can just get through the legal and emotional trial ahead, you will know exactly how to do it correctly...the next time.

You promise that to yourself.

If you're smart, you'll keep that promise.

If you're honest, you will admit you were not really prepared.

And if you are lucky, your first major trial would have been as second-chair to an experienced litigator who was able to teach you some of the procedures, show you some of the moves, and point out some of the pitfalls.

But even the wisest, most experienced, most thorough of teachers, cannot reveal the anxiety of the night before your first opening statement.

And whether you are second-chair or lead counsel, you will know you were not ready. And you should use that knowledge to be as ready as possible the next time and all the times after that. Because—and this is no understatement—a courtroom trial is nothing less than a six-dimensional merry-go-round-jigsaw-puzzle-demolition-derby all playing out in your mind while you sit relatively passively at counsel table, trying to concentrate on 12 things at once while listening to witness testimony.

It's an awful lot of fun and an awful lot of work.

In fact, it may not be possible to be completely and irrefutably prepared for something as complex and ephemeral as a trial at law. After all, you're busy reacting to the judge's attitude, rallying your witnesses and clients, reading the jury's mood and reactions, handling exhibits, fencing with the opposition, preparing witnesses, drafting and touching up your opening statement and closing argument, and readying your direct and cross-examinations. Truly, there is nothing like a jury trial that requires you to marshal your psychological and intellectual resources, and test them in battle against an adversary dedicated to your destruction or, at the very least, to your coming in second in the contest at hand.

There is nothing like a jury trial to test yourself against an adversary dedicated to your destruction.

The reason you will learn much of what you need to know the night before you stand before your first jury is because that first experience will teach you that the mechanics of trial are prefabricated and rather sedate. In fact, the rituals and cadences of the courtroom are almost banal in their reality. The real terror and drama of trial is mainly inside your mind. And, while the emotional tension might occasionally leak into the proceedings, the turmoil is almost all internal.

The only way to begin to quiet that turmoil, to silence the roaring insecurity that threatens to engulf you, is to be prepared and dedicated to your story. You must believe what you are trying to sell. And if you can't believe the *entire* epic with your whole heart, you must find a section of that drama—even a single line—that inspires you. You must find that life raft in the tossing sea and cling to it, nurse it, and inspire it, to bring you safely through.

It also helps to have some *mean* in you.

I'll give you an example:

I went to school with one of the world's great athletes you never heard of. Even in the 8th Grade, John Force was a colossus—6'3", 225 pounds—when everybody around him was a runty 5'6". Back then, John could run the 100-yard dash in 11-flat, broad-jump 17 feet. He got into college on a football scholarship, and later played a few years for the San Francisco 49ers before dropping out of professional sports. In my opinion, John might have been the best athlete Florida ever produced. How is it you never heard of him? Why was he never All-American? His personality. John was one of the sweetest individuals I ever knew. Pound for pound, he may have been the sweetest person who ever lived. Every bone in his body was good-natured. And to succeed in big time sports—or any intense competition—you need some *mean* in you. John Force had none.

When I say a litigator needs to have some mean, I am talking about intensity, a love of competition, and perhaps a little stubborn streak. After all, you will be standing up for a party about whom your opposition and his Paid Forces of Evil will be saying uncomplimentary things. Simply being "nice" won't carry the day, although professional courtesy, honesty, and calmness are always encouraged.

You need not be mean in the same sense that meanness is required to prevail in a physical contest. *But you need to have a reservoir of righteous indignation.* Even if your entire case seems to be a hopeless mess, you must find that one fact, one piece of evidence, one bit of testimony, that justifies your showing up in court, and you must invest yourself and your case in that point. You must be able to drag that righteous indignation from inside you and pour it over the jury as if it were holy water. If you cannot, you are lost.

It helps to have a little mean in you; a reservoir of righteous indignation.

The key is finding that point.

If you have a strong case, there will be many such elements. But even in the weakest case, there will be at least one…or you must convince yourself there is. As we discussed in the section on the Settlement Negotiations (Chapter 15), there is in every case a high point, even if it is a relatively low high point. And in every dispute there is a story you can tell, and you must wholeheartedly believe in that story, because if you don't the jury won't either.

Interestingly, the experts are, well, expert at finding the strongest point in their presentation, and relying on that to wash over all opposing points. Having observed this technique used by many persuasive expert witnesses, I started adopting it for my fact witnesses. Now, I prepare my witnesses by asking them to contemplate the most important truth they want to relate, and to use that truth to deflect questions they are embarrassed to answer or that they think unfair or misleading. If asked, "*Did you inspect the bleed valve prior to beginning your welding activities?*", you could say, "*No.*" Or...you could say, "*The company foreman is responsible for checking the valve.*" Now that answer might be followed by a lot of lawyer barking and objections and righteous indignation at the "non-responsiveness" of the answer, but the witness' point will have been made. They are not defenseless. They will not be pushed around.

You must walk into court with this same attitude.

A COURT'S OBSERVATIONS FOR ATTORNEYS

By The Honorable William P. Barry

Be on time and be prepared. That's the No. 1 Rule, and the rest of the rules follow from that admonition:

Give thought to what you're asking the judge to read. If you throw your papers together on the assumption the judge won't read them, what makes you think that same judge will listen to, and understand, your oral argument? Face it, the best and perhaps only time you can grab the judge's attention is with your written work, which the judge, or the law clerk will review before the hearing.

Simplify the decision-making process. Use an approach known by the acronym "KISS" (keep it simple, stupid). KISS works for juries, too. Ask yourself, *"Am I presenting the information and arguments in a manner that helps the judge to rule in my favor?"* This approach is especially useful when drafting a brief. Assume the judge has many pending cases, and does not know your case like you do. Remember, too, the court's file is a public record. So, it may be in a state of disarray even if it is complete. For your brief, use a short introduction to orient your reader to the facts of the case and the relief you seek. Include everything you want the judge to review. Tab or use colored sheets between exhibits; highlight the portion of the exhibit that you want the judge to read, and don't cheat on the page limit and font rules. If exhibits make your brief more than an inch think, file your exhibits separately; lodge a proposed order, and finally, drop a courtesy copy off with the courtroom clerk. The more time spent on your papers the better.

Address adverse facts or law forthrightly. If there is no satisfactory response, concede the point even if it means that you may lose the case. The "day of reckoning" will happen at some point; why put it off? The judge will expect candor, and your reputation will suffer if you try to avoid the inevitable. When you get asked a question, answer the question that was asked not the one you'd rather answer. If you can't answer it, give a concise and frank explanation why you cannot. The judge was a lawyer, too, and can recognize an evasive or non-responsive reply as well as you can. This is not a time for whining.

Consider the time demands placed on the judge. While the judge is on the bench, paperwork in chambers piles up. Therefore, any delays are going to be annoying. Do you want your decision-maker to be annoyed with you? Your peers may have little choice but to live with tardiness, or lack of preparation. But the judge does not, and neither does the jury. Direct your comments and argument to the person whose decision counts—the judge, not your opponent. This also tends to keep respective emotions in check.

Know when to fold your tent. When the decision has been made, it's final whether or not the judge is correct. Be courteous and accept the decision (judges do not appreciate haggling). The best you can hope to salvage at this point is a clear record for appeal, and your reputation for professionalism. If you are in the middle of a witness's examination, just ask for time to make your offer of proof at the next break.

No two judges handle their courtrooms the same. Many judges provide information about their courtroom practices and preferences. Call the courtroom clerk before you make your first appearance, and ask if this information is available and how you can access it. You can rest assured that if you are curt, rude or dismissive in your dealings with the court's staff, the judge will hear about it. You might, too, and it won't be pretty.

Resolve the dispute. When the court rules require that you meet and confer to resolve a dispute, you are expected to actually speak with one another to try to resolve the dispute. Letters fired back and forth like salvos in a naval engagement are not a "discussion," and are not a good faith effort to deal with the dispute. For example, discovery disputes can often be handled by a middle ground position, with each side retaining the right to seek relief from the court later on with respect to the matters which remain in dispute. Think about how reasonable your position on the motion to compel discovery will look if you offered a compromise before the judge was asked to get involved.

Judge Barry presides in California Superior Court for the County of Los Angeles.

CHAPTER 20

What Verdicts Teach

Law school was a trial. Practice is a trial. And some of our cases will end in trial. And, as I noted at the beginning of this book, the verdict in any trial will be a judgment of the attorneys who conducted that trial.

And sometimes that judgment will be that you...lose.

You may have lost because you were ill-prepared.

You can lament those other responsibilities that robbed you of the time needed to have digested all the facts and documents to best advantage; you can curse your client's failure to lend more helpful assistance; you can chafe at the pressure applied by the court to force the case to trial prematurely; and you can resent the judge's erroneous and unfair rulings on evidence. In sum, you can find lots of reasons to explain your failure. Or, depending on the reason you lost, you can simply admit your failure and resolve never to allow the same thing to happen again.

You may have lost because you were not persuasive enough.

Again, you can blame outside forces working against you, or you can dedicate yourself to falling more deeply in love with the next case you take to trial. For that is the key to persuasion—not only righteous indignation, but also profound and real respect for your client's position. That respect will inform your every question, every gesture, every objection, every argument to the jury, and that is the key to persuasion. Snake oil salesmen are persuasive not because they are without dignity; they are persuasive because they convinced themselves of the efficacy of their product. They can sell it to you because they believe in it themselves.

You may have lost because the facts and the law favor the other side.

Opposing counsel may have every bit as much faith in his or her cause and, in addition, the more believable witnesses, and the more compelling evidence. If you followed the advice shared earlier in this book, you would have analyzed those cases thoroughly and accurately, and cut the best settlement deal you could in a losing situation. You would not have taken that case to trial. Or, if settlement is impossible, you would have prepared your client for the loss and set a reserve that was near the final result. Remember, if you lose a million dollars when you should have lost five million, you haven't been *hit*, that's a victory!

Most cases are lost because the facts and the law favor the other side.

BACK STORY #1

Some day there will come a case when you find you do not have control.

In my own case, an important witness—the manager of a company I was defending—after testifying at deposition that he had six years experience in the industry before he was hired, blurted out on the witness stand at trial that he actually had only six months experience and had lied to get the job.

If he had simply told the truth at deposition, no one would have even noticed. His experience had nothing to do with the case; it was a non-factor. But after he had first lied to get the job, and then had subsequently lied in his deposition, he ultimately decided he could not lie from the witness stand. And that was the end of my defense. Although I tried to rehabilitate the witness by asking him about his financial distress, his need for work, his exemplary record in his four years at the company, the levee had been breached, and the flood waters swallowed up the entire case and me with it. This witness admitted he was a liar and the rest of his testimony was discounted.

At best, the company he represented was seen as incompetent. It could not even hire its personnel carefully and competently. It was, apparently, incapable of performing a basic check of work experience, and so careless it didn't think that was necessary. At worst, the company was seen as a den of thieves, tramps, and liars.

Afterwards I asked this young man—a generally decent fellow—why he decided to reveal the truth in open court, and why he hadn't told me earlier. He said he didn't know, and from the look in his eyes I knew his answer on the stand was as great a mystery and source of bewilderment to him as it was to me. He could lie under oath in deposition, but not in the Courtroom. And that's just the way it was.

That's why you must realize, that even when you have given your best, you are going to lose some cases.

How do attorneys deal with losing?

Some abuse drugs, some quit the profession or, at least, any adversarial aspect of legal practice, and some end up hiding or destroying evidence, lying to the Court and opposing counsel, paying witnesses for favorable testimony and otherwise degrading themselves and the profession. They have forgotten that, at the bar, you win whenever you have done your job to the best of your ability ethically and conscientiously. Losing does not make you a bad person, or a bad attorney, even if you think you might have or should have done something differently, worked harder, been more clever. You are a problem-solving machine designed to create solutions to legal problems, and then you must divorce yourself from that result.

So, whether a case goes to trial over a two-company merger that falls apart, or a shrimp boat that is run over and sunk by an ocean barge, or an offshore oil platform that explodes, it is what it is. You move on. After all, you have 11 other files on your desk that really need your attention.

You are going to lose some cases even when you have given your best.

BACK STORY #2

When it comes to mistakes, your efforts should be directed at anticipating the problem areas and minimizing errors rather than being paranoid about making them.

My natural tendency, of course, is to deny making mistakes, and claim that every apparent error was, in fact, a ruse designed by me to lull the opposition into thinking, erroneously, it had the upper hand.

But it just wasn't so when it came to my biggest legal error.

It occurred while filing a cross-complaint against an insurance company that was affiliated with the insurance company I represented in a complex casualty involving the destruction of an ocean barge-mounted crane worth several million dollars. The reason for my error—as is every such mistake—was bad lawyering. I was completely convinced of the rectitude of my client's position. I knew that the company which prepared the crane barge for towing to a harbor work site, and which used its own tugs to transport the barge, was responsible when the crane was run into a bridge, causing extensive damage to the bridge, not to mention the destruction of the crane.

I reported all facts, evidence, and theories of liability as clearly and directly as I could so my client was well informed and, I thought, aware of and in total agreement with my intentions. Those intentions were obvious. I was going to bring a cross-claim against the tow boat company. But I failed to specifically request authority to file against the towing company which I knew to be insured by a certain insurance giant which, in turn, I should have known was related to the insurance company I represented, the one which insured the crane barge.

Had I requested express authority to proceed, I learned later, I would have been told to desist and abandon all claim against the tow boat company, the insurance giant preferring to let its smaller subsidiary take the loss on its ledger rather than the giant's own. Instead, in good faith and on firm legal ground, I went ahead and filed against the tow boat company, a claim I was later required to withdraw. In the bargain, I lost a client.

If I had known the exact relationship between the insurers, I would not have acted without the express agreement of my principal. But that begs the point. If I had requested explicit authority to proceed, I would have learned the exact nature of that relationship and, more importantly, avoided embarrassment for my principal and myself.

At its core, my error was steeped in communication egocentrism, a belief that everyone or, in this case, my principal, knows and understands what I know and understand. I assumed my client had read my reports, understood my analysis of liability, and knew the tow boat company was in my sights, and that I was preparing to blast it out of the water (legally speaking). In that assumption, I was mistaken.

On winning

As bad as it is to lose, winning is not always so easy.

In fact, I have walked away from victories and felt worse than when I had lost!

In even the greatest "victories," there is a sense of accomplishment and a sense of loss at the same time. Because, if you are honest, you realize the victory was probably as much or more a result of facts and circumstances that occurred long before you became involved, and which prepared the ground for your accomplishment, perhaps even far beyond the positive effect you had. But as with losing, if you have represented your client ethically and well, you have genuine cause for pride and satisfaction.

At the conclusion of Chapter One, I made a point of saying that the results of a trial at law are as much a verdict on the actions of counsel as any other single factor. Always remember, however, you were not alone. If you represent a plaintiff, especially a personal injury plaintiff, and you score a big result, your pleasure at having prevailed, and at garnering a big payday for your client and yourself, should be tempered by the knowledge that your client underwent physical and emotional trauma and, often, a great deal of pain and anxiety, to ensure your "victory."

If you represent a defendant, you may sometimes gain a "victory" that allows your client, perhaps a large and vastly wealthy corporation, to walk away from a crushed little company or, worse, a crushed person, without paying a cent. Your work persuaded a jury that your client was not liable for any damages and almost assuredly, it was not at fault, for juries will seize almost any rationale to compensate a "victim." But the joy of your victory ought to be tempered knowing there is someone out there suffering, probably all the more so because they were led by another lawyer to believe they would prevail and be showered with riches. Far better for their counsel to have been realistic in their evaluation and to have persuaded them to have taken your settlement offer, even though it may have seemed scant in relation to the alleged injury and certainly in relation to plaintiff's dreams of wealth.

Temper your victory knowing your client underwent trauma, pain, and anxiety.

BACK STORY #3

I consider one of my most satisfying "victories" a case that I settled *before* trial, a case that I was convinced I could win easily and get a defense verdict.

The lawsuit involved an alleged injury on an offshore oil production platform, an unwitnessed fall on a Monday morning, allegedly the result of an unsafe condition. My investigation, however, revealed plaintiff was actually injured in a fight the day before. Generally, I am not sympathetic to people who try to game the system. So, at an early status conference, I was prepared to let plaintiff's counsel know, without revealing my information or its source, that his case was not what he thought. But, then, who shows up at that status conference but plaintiff himself, a very rare event. And who does he bring with him but his four-year-old son, a leukemia patient.

I eventually persuaded my principals, a major oil company and their insurer, that they could pay me to defend the lawsuit through trial, probably to a good result, but they would be better served by taking the money they would have paid me and putting it into a settlement pot. With that fund, I told them, I would make certain the file was closed quickly. Looking back at 25 years of winning verdicts, positive legal results, and excellent settlements—representing both plaintiffs and defendants—I still consider that rather average settlement to be one of my great victories.

EPILOGUE

Who Will Train Tomorrow's Litigators?

For some time, the overriding theme in professional development has been "on-the-job training" starting, almost always in defense firms, with a year or two in the law library, where research and writing hours can be billed without hesitation. Even in a plaintiff's personal injury practice where fees are based on a percentage of any recovery, and more of a premium is placed on lucrative production, new associates learn the ropes by handling paper discovery and basic research.

For many firms, the entire training and professional development program consists of little more than assigning a new associate to a team with a leader whose excellence is so manifest and obvious and, seemingly, so contagious, the associate is expected to absorb the leader's abilities automatically by means of observation and osmosis. Occasionally, attorneys might be required to participate in the legal equivalent of a construction crew "tail gate" meeting in-house once a month or so to discuss some aspect of the law or practice.

Other firms underwrite their attorneys' participation in programs which are provided by third parties in the form of continuing legal education (CLE) seminars, mandatory in most states. But CLE sessions are tolerated merely as a necessary evil by most attendees, and rarely, if ever, are they very effective in imparting more than the basics of any particular area of interest. If, for example, you know nothing about immigration law, and are too lazy to wander down to the law library for a couple of hours to find out, a CLE class might provide you with a binder of background material and a few tips on where to begin. Too frequently, though, the workshops are boring, self-promoting exercises with little content of value.

One large law firm I know had a formal associate training and mentoring program in place for many years. In the space of six years it first abandoned the program in favor of one-to-one mentoring from partners and senior associates on the "team" to which the juniors had been assigned, and then returned to a formal program because its "team training" was uneven at best and non-existent at worst. The firm finally abandoned the program again when it was thought that too many potentially billable hours were being lost to training. Soon after, the firm ended up dissolving the partnership.

The firm's dissolution was perhaps only indirectly related to its training and mentoring issues but reflects a larger reality.

Associates are too valuable billing hours on specialized projects or accomplishing certain types of repeated procedures or pounding out the hours on a few major files, to spare for generalized training in the theory and practice of law.

After all, is an associate better off doing legal research and writing briefs on arcane points of law to satisfy a senior partner's curiosity and calm his fears that he might be overlooking a crucial bit of the law that favors his client? Or, is she better off trailing along as a partner goes about her day in Court, in the boardroom of a major client, and in the library? Look at it this way: Which activity is easiest to bill and more easily justified to the client? Then ask yourself which is the more important issue: Value to the firm in terms of immediate income, or value to the associate and, *perhaps*, to the firm and its clients, but only in the long term, in regard to training and professional development?

The answer, as you may have guessed, is the reason why many firms, including many large, profitable enterprises, have reduced if not abandoned their formal, organized programs to train and instruct young lawyers.

The profession has spawned a class of practitioners who can "do" a great deal, but who cannot conceptualize their goals, actions or purpose.

What is really lost, however, is the value of a mentor, a senior whose door is open to the young, and even the more experienced attorney, looking to stretch out in an easy chair, describe a sticky issue in a case, and fish for new ideas and perspectives; not necessarily for the "right" answer or even an effective way to "handle" the situation, i.e., the way it was done the last time a similar situation arose. Surely both the "right" answer and the best previous answer may provide food for thought on the topic at hand. The true need, however, is not simply for a course of action but for a method of thinking and problem-solving and a sounding board for new ideas.

The loss of the true mentor means the loss of creativity.

The legal profession (along with many other modern professions including, most especially, the scientific fields), has spawned a class of practitioner who can "do" a great deal, but who cannot conceptualize their actions or purpose. Interestingly, in scientific fields, taking action without knowing why is often sufficient. As my daughter's pediatrician once told me, *"It's been so long since I did the research, I forget why I prescribe this medication for this condition. But I've been doing it for 30 years now, and it always works."* And it did work. So that was all we needed.

The loss of the true mentor means the loss of creativity.

But unlike medicine, law is not a field where the problem is a rash or a wheeze that will either get worse or be cured.

In the practice of law, one must consider the intricate legal and psychological relationships of perhaps a number of different persons or corporate entities. In any legal contest the variables will occasionally be so numerous as to seem infinite, and competing parties will often be at bitter odds over how to accomplish a goal that, paradoxically, both sides claim to desire above all else, that being a reasonable conclusion. In these circumstances, knowing how to "do" without knowing how to "think" creates a gap that is filled with ineffective representation, unnecessary work, stress, hostility, and resentment, all of which are reflected—as any judge will attest—in declining standards of professionalism, an endemic lack of civility, and increased public dissatisfaction with the entire system of justice which has been and should be one of the pillars of this democracy.

Appendix

A SAMPLE REPORT TO CLIENT

October 17, 2012

Ms. Sophia J
World Claims Adjusters
11707 Wilshire Avenue
Los Angeles, CA

Re: X Industries v. ABC Ins. Co. & Broker
Your Ref: 123 A 398
Our Ref: 2157 06 2373

Dear Ms. J:

On Motion of co-defendant ABC Ins. Co., the Court has continued Trial of this matter until 21 June 2013. The final Pre-Trial Conference is scheduled for 10 June 2013.

FACTS

Our client Broker provided Property coverage to X Industries through ABC Ins. Co. The policy was a standard property form with the ususal terms and conditions and exclusions for product loss or damage due to defective workmanship or deterioration not due to external, fortuitous causes. In brief, the coverage extends to property damaged or destroyed by an accidental casualty such as fire, flood, building collapse and the like but not against simply making a bad product. X Industries, having allegedly lost its regular supplier of a resin component for its plastic products, used an inappropriate substitute resulting in the rapid deterioration of the goods produced. X Industries has brought suit against ABC Ins. Co. and Broker claiming its Property policy should cover the alleged loss of $700,000.00 worth of product and over $6 million in lost business. Additional claims are raised against Broker, our assured, for professional negligence and failure to obtain proper coverage.

<u>SUMMARY</u>

I expect defendant ABC Ins. Co. to be dismissed at hearing on its Motion for Summary Judgment on calendar for December 12, 2012. Similarly, I do not believe Broker has significant exposure to liability as an insurer, that is, in place and instead of ABC Ins. Co. On the other hand, Plaintiff's claims for professional negligence against Broker for "failing to meet the standard of care required of brokers" is a fact driven question which may force this case to trial.

Damages are claimed to be over $700,000.00 for unusable product and $6 million in loss of profit and diminution in value of X Industries as a result of the product loss. Based on the scant documentation produced to date, I calculate the actual recoverable value of the defective product to be approximately $250,000.00

With your authority, we have made a nuisance value offer in an attempt to open a settlement negotiation. We await a counter demand from Plaintiffs.

<u>LITIGATION STATUS</u>

A stay on discovery had been in effect until lifted by the Court on 19 August 2012. The stay was instituted while the Court was considering ABC Ins. Co.'s Motion for Judgment on the Pleadings which, if successful, would have resulted in an immediate determination there was no coverage under the property policy. ABC Ins. Co.'s Motion was based on language within the four corners of the policy and did not refer to any act of our assured, Broker, as having an impact on its coverage determination. Thus, had the Motion been granted, we could have moved immediately for partial dismissal of the Complaint on the grounds that no act of our assured affected coverage. A copy of the ABC Ins. Co. Motion is enclosed.

At hearing, the Court ruled on a technicality that grounds did not exist to permit the subject policy to be admitted into evidence. ABC Ins. Co. counsel had offered the company's form policy as the controlling document. Plaintiffs' counsel refused to agree the form policy was applicable, insisting a certified copy of the actual policy must be submitted. Because Plaintiffs' position was, technically, correct, the Motion was denied.

Immediately after the discovery stay was lifted, counsel for Plaintiffs filed a Notice of Unavailability for a six week period beginning on August 29, 2012. Thus, there was little activity through August and September beyond the filing of Oppositions and Replies to pleadings previously filed by ABC Ins. Co. and Plaintiffs.

Now that discovery is open, we have noticed the deposition of Plaintiff X Industries' Person Most Qualified to testify as to various aspects of the claim. A copy of our Notice is enclosed. We have obtained the agreement of counsel for ABC Ins. Co. to share equally in the costs of this deposition which, at the request of Plaintiffs' counsel, has been scheduled for 18 January 2013. I have also noticed the depositions of Stan and Anna P, individual Plaintiffs herein and the principals of X Industries. As Stan P is designated the corporate representative to be deposed on 18 January, however, those depositions will be taken later.

In the interim, counsel for ABC Ins. Co. has propounded discovery aimed at having the subject policy admitted into evidence as well as for documents and information concerning the alleged loss and calculation of damages. I believe the Request for Production appended to our Notice of Deposition should be effective in obtaining, at the earliest date, all available documentation relating to the alleged loss. Based on the conduct of plaintiffs' counsel to date, however, I expect the responses to our document request may be unhelpful if not totally evasive. For that reason, I believe the best chance of creating a record of plaintiffs' knowledge, actions and intentions will come through the deposition itself.

If complete and proper documentation is not produced, it may be necessary to proceed with discovery motions to compel production. Because X Industries was sold by the P's subsequent to bringing suit, I would not be surprised for X to claim they are no longer in possession of documents relating to the loss. At that point, we would have to depose the Person Most Qualified at K Corp., the purchaser of X Industries and a third party to this action. How much cooperation we would receive from K Corp. is an open question.

As you know, we had been maintaining a low profile, allowing ABC Ins. Co. to take the laboring oar and present itself as the larger target. I believe it is now apparent we must become more active to protect our assured Broker in anticipation of ABC Ins. Co. being able to extricate itself via Motion for Summary Judgment, a more likely result than not, if my reading of the Court's comments at the latest hearing are accurate.

LIABILITY

Like many cases which, at first glance, seem to be readily defensible based on simple common sense, there is not a large body of law which directly addresses the issues raised here. Most decisions dealing with defective products arise from traditional, third party, product liability claims, not claims for failure to procure coverage for "defective manufacture." Over time, and several appearances testing legal issues, we believe we have been able to persuade the Court that no such insurance coverage exists. We have taken every opportunity to point out that if it did, no manufacturer would have a vested interest in quality control or anything more than the most rudimentary, and cheap, production standards because the maker could be guaranteed, at least, the recovery of their investment from insurance if they should put a defective or inferior product on the market.

In the case of Parallax Productions v. Pancoast Underwriting, 16 Cal. App 4th 333 (2004), the Court, while also addressing third party liability issues, determined that general liability insurance which responded to a claim against the manufacturer for sale of a defective product would cover property damaged by the product but did not cover the product itself. It is noteworthy, however, that this decision treated a CGL policy which is directed at liability to third parties and not the property of the manufacturer. In the present case, we are dealing with a denial of coverage under a property policy which, in the normal, fortuitous circumstances such as fire and flood, would cover the manufacturer/insured's property.

We have also found cases [e.g., Sympatico Products v. Dynastic Ins. Co., 437 F. Supp. 233 E.D. La (2005)] which allow an insured to recover for damage to an insured's own property caused by other, defectively manufactured property of the insured. In those cases, the Courts generally conclude that, as the manufacturer did not intend to produce a defective product, the damage to the separate property was accidental and, thus, covered by the insurance. These cases, however, do not address the issue of whether the coverage extends to the defectively produced product itself.

While we believe that, ultimately, the Court will determine there is no coverage for the loss, it is the professional negligence and breach of implied contract claims against our insured that are more troublesome. The principal of X Industries claims he was told by our insured's broker/agent that he was "fully covered" for any and all possible losses. Based on this assurance, he claims he purchased all the insurance recommended by our Broker, without question, because he thought X Industries was protected against any loss. Our agent denies these assertions noting no broker could or would guarantee coverage for any eventuality and, moreover, the "defective manufacture" insurance X Industries says it was promised, simply does not exist.

DAMAGES

The damages claimed are substantial. X Industries states it had to destroy and discard over $700,000.00 worth of stock consisting of valves and hoses. Moreover, it claims the defective product was returned by customers who cancelled orders and severed business relationships all of which impacted its business adversely to the extent of $6 million. Based on the scant documentation provided to date, it appears the gross revenues of X Industries totaled $1.6 million in the last tax year. At the same time, a review of other financial records seems to indicate X Industries showed no profit, and paid no taxes, for the same period.

Setting aside any issues of liability, there is no doubt X Industries suffered losses as a result of its manufacture and distribution of the defective product. On the other hand, X Industries calculates its loss based on sales price while, under applicable law, it would be entitled to recover, at most, only the fair market value of its property as produced, i.e., its cost of manufacture. Based on available records, we estimate this out-of-pocket loss to be approximately $250,000.00.

As for its claim for loss of business and diminution of corporate value, it is clear X Industries depended on rather creative accounting practices to avoid showing an annual profit. Thus, it will have a difficult time supporting its $6 million claim. We must anticipate, however, that the retained experts of X Industries will make a showing at trial that the value of the company is not restricted to profit but more directly related to gross revenues, good will, potential sales and other factors which would tend to support a multi-million dollar claim.

SETTLEMENT

As per our agreed plan, because Plaintiffs' counsel was unwilling to make a demand, we have made an opening offer of $10,000.00. Counsel advised he would respond in a timely manner. To date there has been no response. I am of the view that plaintiff's counsel realizes, even though the Court overruled the Motion for Judgment on the Pleadings, that the Court seems persuaded there is no coverage under the policy. Thus, counsel has come to believe plaintiff's only case will be against Broker for "failure to procure proper insurance." For that reason, plaintiff's settlement position, at least in the short term, will likely become more firm and, perhaps, unrealistic.

<u>STRATEGY</u>

I expect plaintiffs' testimony at deposition will proclaim X Industries was assured by Broker that if X Industries made a defective product, as in this case, coverage would be provided. The fact that no such coverage exists, and common sense suggests that, if it did, no business would ever fail and no company would have any incentive to produce merchantable goods, does not seem to register with plaintiff's counsel. I believe, however, we have been more successful in getting this point to register with the Judge. Thus, as soon as X 's Person Most Qualified is deposed, I intend to obtain an expert declaration, as well as declarations from Broker personnel, to present this issue to the Court in the form of a Motion for Summary Judgement or, in the Alternative, Summary Adjudication on the issue of coverage.

I expect we shall prevail on the coverage issue. That is, the Court will not find a "breach of contract" requiring Broker to stand in the shoes of ABC Ins. Co. to provide the claimed coverage. And it should, therefore, be easier to win the contest over whether or not such coverage was ever promised. Plaintiffs may claim, however, logic and law to the contrary, they were assured by Broker there would be such coverage. The most simple way for the Court to rule would be to note this as a disputed issue of fact to be determined at trial and, thus, deny that portion of the Motion. This is the result I expect. While we should consider carefully whether to undertake the expense of the Motion given the low probability of complete success. I do believe the Motion would be effective in further educating our generally competent and knowledgeable Judge as to some of the realities of insurance coverage. Further, this could be valuable both in pressing our case to Plaintiffs' counsel during settlement negotiations and, if we are to proceed to trial, helping to ensure the Judge's logic and sentiments will be with the defense.

Legal research I have conducted in the area shows the rulings in suits against brokers in similar cases to be fact driven. That is, while no duty exists for a broker to ensure that every possible claim presented to underwriters will be covered, if an affirmative representation is made by the broker promising coverage, then a failure to procure the promised coverage is a breach of the duty assumed. As noted, while I expect plaintiffs to stop short of admitting they intended to make a defective product (and, thus, specifically warned the Broker what claims they expected to make), I believe they will be coached to come as close as possible to stating they raised the possibility of that scenario in describing their dealings with Broker and requests for insurance coverage.

As you may surmise, I do not hold plaintiffs' counsel in high regard. I would not be surprised if Stan P was coached to testify that he knew products could sometimes be made with improper components, despite the most strenuous testing, and so Broker was asked to protect X Industries in such a circumstance. Of course, a witness willing to bend the truth always has the necessary testimony available to support his case. I fear we are facing such individuals in this case. The result will be a classic "swearing contest" with Stan P swearing he asked Broker for the equivalent of product defect coverage even if not in those words. Broker's agents will swear no such request was made nor any assurance given because, among other reasons, such insurance does not exist.

<u>DEPOSITION OF JOHN DOE, CPA</u>

Doe has been X Industries' accountant for three years. He is qualified and well experienced although his academic and professional background are not especially distinguished. Moreover, Doe appeared to be a somewhat reluctant witness. It might be suspected that, having assisted X Industries in understating the company's profits, perhaps for tax reasons, he may now be uncomfortable supporting the huge claim for the value of the business.

In general, Doe testified in accordance with his written records including the company's profit and loss statements previously analyzed and reported to you. His one significant point of departure from those reports concerned the accounting procedures for capital investment in research and development. Doe now concedes that the unusually large write-offs for the purchase of testing equipment might have been made in error as he has "recently discovered" the equipment was actually leased, not purchased. He explains this "error" occurred because the amounts stated are accurate but would have been payable only if the subject equipment had been lost or damaged. In fact, the lease payments actually made amount to less than 9 percent of the write-off taken as an expense. This error alone reduces the claimed value of the business by almost 50 percent.

EXPERTS

I think it is becoming increasingly likely this case will proceed to trial. If settlement is accomplished, I expect it will come shortly before trial. Accordingly, expert testimony will be required to describe the duties and obligations of a broker as well as the meaning, function and purpose of property and liability insurance. There will be no other means of getting such evidence before the trier of fact.

I have worked in the past with a well-experienced insurance expert in claims handling and coverage matters and am familiar with two other experts, both in Orange County, who can testify regarding a broker's duties and the types and intent of various coverages. Those individuals, who I believe are known to you, are Cynthia T. and Eliot R. I will be speaking with them this week regarding their fees and retainers. Before making a selection, I will consult with you to discuss estimates of their charges and my recommendation. Of course, if you have a suggestion as to designation of another expert, I would welcome your recommendation. I do prefer local experts, to avoid the "hired gun" implications to the jury, but an imminently well-qualified and well spoken expert, even if not local, would be certainly be positive and could outweigh a "local" connection.

BUDGET

I propose the following budget for your consideration. Of course, these parameters are only estimates but I would expect the final figure to be close to this total. I trust you will find these estimates to be appropriate and complete.

LEGAL

Fact Investigation/Reporting	hrs.	$
Analysis/Strategy	hrs.	$
Pleadings	hrs.	$

Court Mandated Conferences	hrs.	$
Dispositive Motions	hrs.	$
Other Written Motions	hrs.	$
Written Discovery	hrs.	$
Document Production	hrs.	$
Depositions	hrs.	$
Mediation	hrs.	$
Expert Discovery	hrs.	$
Discovery Motions	hrs.	$
Legal Research	hrs.	$

TRIAL

Preparation	hrs.	$
Fact Witnesses	hrs.	$
Expert Witnesses	hrs.	$
Written Motions	hrs.	$
Exhibit Preparation	hrs.	$
Jury Instructions	hrs.	$
Meet and Confer	hrs.	$
Other Trial Preparation	hrs.	$
Trial (five days)	hrs.	$
Verdict Form/Judgement	hrs.	$
Post Trial Motions	hrs.	$

EXPENSES

Experts Fees	hrs.	$
Mediators/Arbitrators	hrs.	$
Deposition Transcripts	hrs.	$
Trial Transcripts	hrs.	$
Trial Exhibits	hrs.	$
Court Fees	hrs.	$
Subpoenas (service)	hrs.	$
Witness Fees	hrs.	$
Local Travel	hrs.	$

Out of Town Travel	hrs.	$
Courier & Messenger	hrs.	$
Photocopies	hrs.	$
Printing	hrs.	$
Online Research	hrs.	$
TOTAL		$

We shall, of course, continue to monitor this action closely and report significant events to you.

Very truly yours,
Martin L. Grayson

SAMPLE COVER SHEET

COVER SHEET

Re:	Affiliated Corp. v. Systems, Inc. et al. Crane Collapse/Port of Los Angeles 6/10/12 Our Ref: 0287 10 5017	
Report To:	Mr. Ralph Kramden Affiliated Corporation 10700 Coastal Way Los Angeles, CA 90888	Your ref: LA 11 WP 271
Tel:	(310) 505-xxxx (310) 868-xxxx (310) 367-xxxx	
Fax:	(310) 505-xxxx	

Your ref: LA 06 WP 271

U.S. District Court – Central District of California   Docket No. CV 765 238
312 North Spring Street
Los Angeles, CA 90010

Hon. Egbert A. Souse
Clerk: William Dunkenfield (213) 206-xxxx
Court Reporter: Amadeo Avogadro (213) 206-xxxx

Edwin Bunt, Esq.   Attorney for Systems
Walther & Bunt, LLP
1200 South Figueroa Street
Los Angeles, CA 90016

Tel: (213) 426-xxxx
Fax: (213) 426-xxxx

Gentleman Jim   Marine Surveyor
Oceans Away, Ltd.
1660 Water Crest Ste 300
Long Beach, CA 90802

Tel: (562) 498-xxxx
Fax: (562) 498-xxxx

MEMORANDUM

Your office should have a procedure memo for each distinct legal operation. The goal of each such memo is to describe the action required in such a clear and precise manner that a temporary employee could pick up the memo and successfully complete the operation without further instruction. Here is our general procedure for handling defense files. Needless to say, any particular action such as preparing and filing a Motion for Summary Judgment, for example, would require additional oversight and perhaps instruction by a senior attorney.

MEMORANDUM

TO: **Staff**
DATE: **November 30, 2012**
RE: **Defense Handling Procedures**

1. Acknowledge assignment of the file to client.
2. Obtain an extension of time in which to Answer, if necessary.
3. Obtain authority from client to associate an investigator, if necessary. (Explain why it is necessary and ask for their recommendation. If none, confirm authority to select one.)
4. Do legal research on defenses.
5. Engage investigator and confirm by letter with requirements.
6. File an Answer, if necessary.
7. Report to client with Answer.
8. Propound discovery to plaintiff and co-defendants.
9. Notice deposition of plaintiff and co-defendants.
10. Obtain reports (medical, loss, accident, investigation, etc.) from plaintiff.
11. Engage experts, if necessary.
12. Depose witnesses.
13. Depose experts of plaintiff, including doctors.
14. Prepare Pre-Trial Order including Witness List, Exhibit List, Statement of Case, etc.
15. Subpoena witnesses, including our own.
16. Arrange transportation, accommodations and preparations of witnesses for trial.

Files\Procedures\Legal\Defense Handling Proc (Revised 11/30/12)

THE PLEADING INDEX

Some attorneys have no file system, others use a three-folder filing system (pleadings, correspondence, all else), and still others use other more or less formal systems. The systems in our office evolved over the years. Even with the extensive use of computers and scanning, however, we like to keep hard copies of all file material. Our correspondence folders are in strict chronological order, from the first item to the present, with the originals filed as is but with the file copy of any item we generate, whether a Report to Client, correspondence, or memorandum, printed on canary yellow paper. That way, at a glance, we can distinguish incoming from outgoing material.

The Pleading Index is a very handy tool, even more so with computers than it was when the Index was the only way to track the Court record. Today, if I'm looking for the Opposition to a Motion, or a Discovery response, rather than looking through thousands, or hundreds, or dozens of documents, all I have to do is bring up my file Pleading Index, do a search for the document title and there it is. In court, the printed, hard copy of the Index, coupled with the number tabs in the Pleading folders, allows me to find any document in very little time.

Our Pleading Index works equally well with 20 pleadings or 2,000. It looks like this:

PLEADING INDEX
VOL. I

CASE NAME:________________________ FILE NO: ____________
COURT:________________________ CASE NO:____________
ADDRESS:________________________ PHONE: ____________

NO	FROM	DESCRIPTION	TO	DATE
1)	PL	Complaint	All	06/10/12
2)	DEF - Sleepy	Answer	PL	07/26/12
3)	DEF - Happy	Answer	PL	08/12/12
4)	PL	Interrogs - Set I	DEF - Sleepy	09/11/12
5)	PL	Req. Production - Set I	DEF - Sleepy	09/11/12
6)	DEF - Happy	Motion / Change of Venue	Happy	09/15/12
7)	PL			
8)	PL			

Acknowledgements

How to Litigate is intended to be a virtual mentor for attorneys.

Thus, it is my honor to thank those talented and accomplished lawyers who were mentors to me. Much of how I think about the practice of law comes directly from their lessons or were the result of my efforts, through observation and analysis, to live up to the standard of professional excellence they exemplified and demanded.

Ron Johnson spent long hours showing me what must be done and how to do it carefully, ethically, and thoroughly. Mike McAlpine taught more by demonstration than by design, but those demonstrations were always informed by creativity and insight. Richard Cozad was always available to provide a sympathetic ear and a thoughtful and encouraging word.

My gratitude goes to my first editor on this project, the funny, intelligent, and adorable Sonya Grayson, my daughter. There were many others who contributed at various stages during the seven years this work has been in progress. They include my good friends and, often, morale officers, Sandy Balick, Dennis and Teri Cammarano, David and Martha Gruning, Naurang and Gail Agrawal, Christian and Pamela Wilson, Ram and Laura Katalan, Philip and Denise Gerson, Dave and Jeanne Carden, and Alberta Samuelson.

I also wish to thank The Honorable William P. Barry, Professor Martin Pritikin, Courtney Fowler and Zachary Miller.

Above all, I am ever grateful to my lovely and amazing wife, Kaoru, for her patience, love, encouragement, and humor.

And, of course, to the one without whom none of this…
my Mom, Natalie.

Made in United States
Orlando, FL
05 November 2026

90281942R00098